# THE BASKETMAKER'S ART

## CONTEMPORARY BASKETS AND THEIR MAKERS

### EDITED BY ROB PULLEYN

**Lark Books**

Asheville, North Carolina

Library of Congress Catalog Card Number: 86-82336

ISBN 0-937274-28-3

Printed in Hong Kong by South China Printing Company.

Book acknowledgements are frequently tests of one's ability to say
"no." So many people are involved in the creation of a book that it
becomes nearly impossible to stop listing them.

This book, however, was primarily the creation of three people
who each employed considerable creative talent and brought to the
project a cooperative spirit and enthusiasm that made the entire
endeavor a joyful experience.

Nancy Orban was the spirit and hand behind the book. She col-
lected, organized and prepared the materials, worked with the artists
and solved the problems.

Ron Zisman studied the artists' work, read their statements, asked
questions and designed the book.

Thom Boswell gathered together the elements and prepared them
for printing, always looking for the untied loose end.

A special thanks, as usual, to Val Ward who took the pressure,
watched the schedule and pointed out the errors.

A book such as this also needs someone whose role it is to actively
contemplate and to offer explanations. Both Shereen LaPlantz and
Lillian Elliott are to be thanked for their willingness to have their
observations committed to print.

Rob Pulleyn

# THE BASKETMAKER'S ART

# CONTENTS

Introduction

2

## Contemporary Baskets and Their Makers

Biographies

162

# Yesterday's Baskets: Tradition and Form

## Shereen LaPlantz

Top left: Tlinget basket, cedar root, false embroidery, separate compartment in lidded "rattle top" with seeds inside, twined.
Top right and bottom: Nootka/Makah, cedar root, grass, twined.

The art basket is a relatively new character in the ongoing tale of basketry, and it has a rich, diverse background to build upon. The craft of basketry has been part of most cultures throughout time. There doesn't appear to be a leader, or a single group that discovered basketry and then taught all the others. Instead, basketry seems to have developed simultaneously throughout the world, at the same and different times. This happened because the techniques are simple enough and obvious enough for anyone to stumble onto . . . and basketry filled a need.

Basketry is a living tradition—it is still being influenced, still changing with each basketmaker. So often we think of a tradition as something that is now preserved in a museum. But traditions need not be so strict that there is no room for change, or that they can't be influenced by a single individual. Today's artistic climate encourages all types of basketry. Many artists are reviving basketry traditions and learning from old artisans, old notes, or museum collections. Although they are trying to accurately duplicate work from the past, sometimes even calling themselves "replicators," their reproductions are achieved through an artist's hands and brain. The creative process is selective—artists, even replicators, make baskets in those styles that appeal to them, using materials and shapes they like. When they teach the tradition, they teach what appeals to them and their students comprise the next generation of artists, making baskets that interest *them*. The selective process continues and the tradition evolves.

To understand the current trends in basketry, let's go back a few hundred years and sketch a brief history. The North American Indian tribes had well-developed basketry traditions before the white settlers arrived, and many of their styles and techniques are still used today. The Pueblo Indians of the Southwest use both coiling and twining techniques. For coiling, their materials range from the rather wide bundles of grasses preferred by the Hopi, to the stiffer, thinner rod coils in the Apache baskets. Yucca leaves and devil's-claw are used for designs worked over core bundles of grasses or shoots. For twining, stiffer materials are used: willow shoots or the more readily available commercial reed. The Southwest is known for intricate motifs on its baskets; human, animal, and kachina designs are used, as well as geometrics.

There was also a high density of Indian tribes in California. The mild climate and availability of food allowed these tribes to develop as smaller groups; these groups in turn created a wide variety of basketry styles. Tribes of southern California work mostly in coiling, using grasses, rush stems, and yucca leaves. Designs are intricate, often geometric, with some human and animal forms. The Pima also use devil's-claw for design work. Some tribes use feathers to decorate the outermost edges of wide bottle forms. Coiling and twining both were used by tribes of central California, as far north as the wine country and Pomo. Their utilitarian seed beaters and fish traps are worked in open twining, and made with stiff shoots of materials such as willow and hazel. Finer twining is used in baskets meant for storage, carrying, and grinding. The patterns are geometric, and quite intricate. The coiling also tends to be finer, over a rod core. These patterns, too, are geometric, but are often decorated with beads, shell pieces, or feathers. The Pomo are also known for their miniature coiled baskets.

The tribes of northern California use a double-strand twining technique that makes a pattern on the outside of the basket, while the interior is left plain. Bear grass, maidenhair fern, and hazel are among the materials used. The patterns are geometric and intricate. The Hoopa Indians of that area make particularly fine basket hats that are simple bowl forms worn upside down on the head.

Tribes of the Pacific Northwest make twined and coiled baskets. Twining seems to be predominant. The Nez Perce make soft, flat bags out of corn husks and yarn. The patterning is geometric, worked as a wide band which covers most of the bag. The Washo make round, soft bags called "Sally bags," which are often decorated with highly stylized human and animal forms. The Tlinget make rattle-top baskets that are especially interesting. Enclosed in the basket's lid is a finial, with seed hulls sealed inside of it. The lid rattles softly when moved.

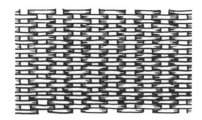

Plain weave. Over 1, under 1, pattern.

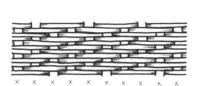

Twill. Over 2, under 1, pattern.

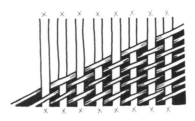

Randing. An over 1, under 1, weave with a new weaver tucked behind each upright or stake.

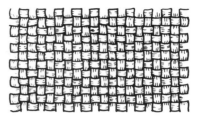

Plaiting. Over 1, under 1, pattern. The difference between plaiting and weaving is the tension. In weaving the stakes are spaced far apart and the weavers closely packed. In plaiting there is even tension between the stakes and weavers, leaving small square openings between the weave.

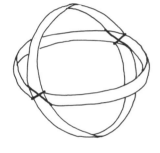

Rib construction. Two hoops are lashed together.

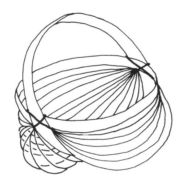

Ribs are added to make a frame. The frame is then woven over.

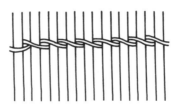

Twining. Twining uses two elements or weavers. They twist around each other as they weave over 1, under 1.

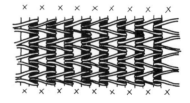

Twining one row with the twist underhand and the next row with the twist overhand.

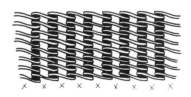

Reverse direction or arrow twining.

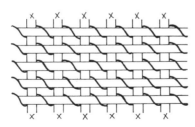

T twining. A rod is placed in front of the stakes and wrapped or lashed in place.

Figure 8 stitch.

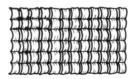

Coiling. The figure 8 stitch always covers the row below it, resulting in a double layer of stitches on each row.

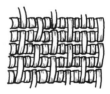

Wrap stitch coiling.

Knotting. The finished look is the same as with figure 8 coiling.

# Traditional Basketry Techniques

Other tribes of the area make finely twined baskets out of cedar root and salt marsh grass. The patterns are delicate, and either geometric or figurative, often depicting people in boats, or whales and fish. The gathering baskets from this area have scalloped, open tops. To enclose the contents securely, a leaf was laid over the open top and laced in place. Coiled baskets from this region are sewn with stiff materials worked over a wide core, and are round or rectangular in shape. The coils are covered with a pleated, flat strip, an imbrication, which carries a geometric design.

The Northern Plains tribes are known for their twined utilitarian baskets, carrying or burden baskets, baby cradles, and seed beaters. These were made from stiff material, shoots and willow, using open and closed twining techniques. The Mandan made woven backpacks with thick U-shaped reinforcing rods at the corners. The patterns on them were geometric.

The area from the Great Lakes to New England comprises the Eastern Woodlands, a region with its own specific styles of basketry. Tribes in this area make baskets of ash splints and sweet grass braids woven together. The pattern work is either in the form of added curlicues of ash, or, in some cases, block-printed geometric designs. The curlicue work is unique to the Eastern Woodland tribes and the eastern Cherokee. The Seneca in this area make masks and mats of braided cornhusks.

The southeastern Indians use cane and palmetto, and work mainly in plaiting. These tribes used designs ranging from simple geometrics to extremely complex geometrics. Some designs were highlighted by the use of three colors; others were executed in a single color, subduing the pattern. The Choctaw made unusually shaped baskets, referred

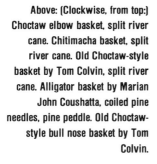

Above: (Clockwise, from top:) Choctaw elbow basket, split river cane. Chitimacha basket, split river cane. Old Choctaw-style basket by Tom Colvin, split river cane. Alligator basket by Marian John Coushatta, coiled pine needles, pine peddle. Old Choctaw-style bull nose basket by Tom Colvin.

Above: New England-style swing handle basket by John E. McGuire, black ash, hickory, double bottom construction.
Left: Shaker fancy basket by John E. McGuire, black ash, hickory.
Photos: Henry E. Peach.

to as "elbow," "bull nose," and "heart." Pine needle coiling also is done in this region by the Coushatta, who often shape their baskets to represent animals, such as alligators and turkeys.

A legend of Louisiana's Chitimacha tribe tells of a valiant warrior who slew a giant serpent that was threatening the tribe. As the serpent writhed in pain before its death, it gouged in the earth a great trough, now the Bayou Teche, where the tribe lives. The warrior's brave deed is still reflected in the distinctive serpentine designs on the double-woven lidded baskets made by the Chitimacha.

Many European immigrants brought their knowledge of basketry techniques and their preferred styles to the United States with them. Frequently they also brought seeds or starts of the basketry materials. As the newcomers settled, their basketry changed, adapting to local needs and materials, the new styles reflecting the influences of their new environment.

The British brought their woven splint baskets, such as market baskets, and willow baskets. The splint baskets have hand-carved handles and are quite sturdy. The Indians probably taught these settlers how to use black and white ash as basketry material.

The Shakers modeled their baskets after the woven ash splint baskets made by the Indians in the area. They worked closely with the Indians and learned from them. The Shakers were concerned with economy of materials, and became adept at working with thinner and thinner splints. Their baskets were made from fresh, green ash, which was formed over molds then left to dry and harden on the mold. This is not an uncommon practice; the Shakers just did it especially well.

5

The Appalachian ribbed baskets seem to be a combination of the Scottish, Irish, German, English, and Indian techniques. There is a controversy over who taught whom, but the resulting basket is a hybrid, different enough to suggest many influences. These baskets are white oak, woven over a rib skeleton. The length and positioning of the ribs dictate the shape of the basket, creating "fanny," "gizzard," "hen," "pie," and "key" baskets, as well as others.

White oak rod baskets also are made in the Appalachian region. The oak is drawn through dies to create thin rods for weaving. Willow work is done here too, as is rye straw coiling.

The Amana Colony, in Iowa, was a cooperative religious community settled by Germans. Each village in the colony had its own basketmaker and willow patch. Apparently there wasn't much interaction between people of Amana with Indians or with other settlers in the area, so their basketry changed little until the 1930's. Some of the basketmakers continued to work at the craft, and have taught their techniques to young basketmakers.

It should be mentioned that willow was—and is—one of the principal materials used for basketry. Willow starts were brought to North America with many of the British and European immigrants, and wil-

low patches can still be found dotting the countryside around older towns. There was even a movement at the end of the 1800's to teach the Indians to use willow for their basketry, but little came of it.

A great deal of willow work is being done today. In the small northern California town where I live, there are willow patches that were started by the Portuguese fishermen who settled here, and wild willow grows by the river. There are still some descendants of the Portuguese who make willow baskets, and there is a Catholic priest here who learned basketry in his native Rumania and still enjoys the craft. Contemporary basketmakers collect wild willow to make art baskets, and there is some willow furniture made here. If you look closely, you'll find that many towns have a similar variety of interest in willow basketry.

The art of basketry was not brought to this country by Europeans alone. The sea islands off South Carolina and Georgia were the first stop in America for many Africans, brought here as slaves. Some stayed on the sea islands, and put their knowledge of basketry to use. These Gullah baskets are made by coiling sea grass. The shapes can be complex, with tiers or undulations. The patterns are kept to simple stripes, and highlight, rather than interfere with, the forms.

**Right:** All Appalachian rib-style white oak baskets. (Clockwise, from top:) "Fanny" or "gizzard" basket with woven rim handle and spine, attributed to Mildred Youngblood. Market basket. Pie basket with woven rim and interior spine, attributed to a cousin of Mildred Youngblood.

**Opposite, top:** (Clockwise, from top:) Round tray, peeled and unpeeled willow by Joanna Schanz. Round Eastern basket, peeled and unpeeled willow with removable rim spikes on the outside by Joanna Schanz. Unpeeled wild willow basket by Joanna Schanz. **Opposite, bottom:** Gullah baskets, coiled sea grass.

This short history of basketry has left out many traditions, glossed over others, and presented only highlights. It is meant only to suggest the richness and diversity of traditions from which contemporary basketmakers learn, and upon which they build. This history is not finished. Immigration continues. New traditions continue to come in, to adapt, and in turn to influence existing traditions. For example, the Southeast Asians and Ethiopians have brought with them their own basketry traditions. They are trying to learn about the basketry materials indigenous to the U.S., and adapt their techniques accordingly. Their work can now be seen in exhibits, and they teach at art centers and weaving supply stores.

The exciting basketry being done today, some of which you will see in this book, has been built on the foundations of past traditions. As artists, we have been influenced by what we see, but this doesn't mean we copy. It means we learn, adding new bits of information to our basketry vocabulary. With enough information we can develop our own styles and make exciting art baskets.

7

Untitled by Katsuhiro Fujimura.
Cut, affixed, piled cardboard,
7'6''x5'3''x8'6'', 7'6''x4'7''x7'9'',
1984. Photo courtesy of 12th
Biennale de la Tapisserie de
Lausanne.

# Today's Baskets:
# The Development of a Contemporary Aesthetic

**Lillian Elliott**

In the beginning, that is, in 7000 B.C., there were baskets, but when I began my career in art in 1960 there were none on the art scene. There were, of course, accomplished native American baskets, but the idea that a basket could be "art" had not yet occurred to anyone besides Ed Rossbach. He exhibited his non-traditional baskets along with other non-loomed textiles in 1968. When his book *Baskets As Textile Art* was published in 1973, the textile community was surprised by it. He did what is popularly called in California "consciousness raising."

Weavers had been searching for larger and larger materials so as to make architecturally scaled textiles, loom woven or not. There was a rather frantic feeling in the air, unnamed but exciting, of a new beginning. Weavers had just begun to think they might be creating art when they made their textiles. That first book of Rossbach's quietly and gently stepped back from the frantic action, and reported in an intimate, personal style on what was going on by observing ethnic baskets. His book was not only an appreciation of past art, but a studied commentary on the current scene. The finite size of baskets was reassuring when the "sculptural" textiles were constantly growing. Not only that, the book showed a broad range of three-dimensional forms constructed using the familiar textile techniques.

In 1976, when Rossbach's *The New Basketry* was published, the audience was there. As a matter of fact, weavers had become so interested in the subject that many of them were *in* the book. From the period when no one made baskets as personal expression to the time when such baskets could barely be presented in a single book had been just a few years. Amazing! It was not only that Rossbach wrote well, it was also that the field of textiles was at an exciting stage. Baskets had entered the textile scene. So had Art.

Jean Lurcat instituted the International Biennial of Tapestry in Lausanne, Switzerland, in 1962 in an effort to develop a greater appreciation of tapestry as an art form. Over the years the Biennial has become a rather prestigious international exhibit, underlining the importance of textiles. One way to trace the development of the art basket is to follow the progression of entries in the Biennial, as they changed from two-dimensional textiles to three-dimensional sculpture. At this point basketry was completely within the fiber world. The Lausanne Biennial was the most celebrated international fiber exhibition. The history of fiber *was* the history of the experimental basketry movement.

The 12th Biennial, in 1985, was titled Textiles as Sculpture. A number of entries related to basketry, but only three could be clearly defined as baskets, and even they used non-traditional materials and methods. One of those entries, Katsuhiro Fujimura's "Untitled" was in fact two enormous baskets constructed of sections of corrugated cardboard, assembled in a most untraditional manner. Anyone who saw these monumental baskets can testify to the potential power inherent in the basket form.

Perhaps the most lasting influence of the Lausanne Biennial has been its effect on the scale of work in textiles, since, until 1985, it required that work be a minimum of five square meters to enter. With this size restriction the Biennial was reinforcing a feeling for size that architects were beginning to look for in textiles. They had begun to seek out large-scale wall hangings to add warmth to the cold, clean architecture of public buildings. New yarns were needed for the larger wall hangings. Traditional fibers, such as wool, linen, and cotton, were available in yarn that was appropriate for the traditional purposes, such as clothing, blankets, and rugs. But when the total size of the work became considerably larger, the scale of the traditional fiber yarns was wrong. Even their feel was not appropriate in the finished work. Wool and cotton, spun so carefully and uniformly to feel good to the wearer, seemed too soft in these "public" textiles. The soft materials were particularly ill-suited to baskets, so the textile artists' search for firmer materials helped the new basketmakers when they began their work. It's worth noting that just when textile artists were hunting hard materials, sculptor Claes Oldenburg was beginning to work in earnest on his soft sculpture, and Christo was wrapping in polyethylene and canvas the fountain at Spoleto and Little Bay, Australia.

Raw fibers filled the need for firmer, larger "yarns." Sisal and jute, rope of all kinds, made an appearance in fiber shows. One exhibit, Deliberate Entanglements, at the UCLA Galleries in 1971, was full of sisal—I know because I'm allergic to it! Textile shows ceased to require that entrants submit three yards of cloth. Large hangings began to protrude from the walls and to be suspended from ceilings. Before long they also were standing in the middle of the room, supported by armatures of steel underneath.

Although the Lausanne Biennial received the most publicity, there were other important international exhibits. Two notable exhibitions of non-functional textiles took place in 1969: Perspectief in Textiel at the Stedelijk Museum in Amsterdam, and Wall Hangings, at the Museum of Modern Art in New York. Perhaps one more backward look is called for: Magdalena Abakanowicz of Poland won a gold medal in 1965 at the Biennial in San Paulo as an *artist* rather than as a fiber artist. And so, hope was instilled in the heart of every ambitious

textile student in this country.

As fiber artists began to "let it all hang out," new artists were beginning to make baskets. At the turn of this century, in his book *Aboriginal American Basketry*, Otis Tufton Mason describes how basketmakers always avail themselves of the materials in their immediate landscape. Some of the basketmakers, in looking for new forms, also looked for new materials. Pointing the way once again was Ed Rossbach, who used newspaper, a readily available fiber on today's landscape, and plastic, a mysterious, durable, and beautiful raw material. His ideas so influenced his students that they were unaware they hadn't always found plastic beautiful.

There are also artists who feel that the harvesting of their own raw materials is crucial to their art. This attitude toward natural materials may reflect a desire to return to simpler, happier times, or may be related to the recent environmental movement, a wish to connect with nature and all living things. Basically, it is the response of individual artists to various natural materials. It is an attitude similar to the response of a traditional craftsman to his material described in this touching passage from the book *Bamboo* (John Weatherhill, Inc.), which tells of a Japanese shakuhachi (flute) maker.

> This maker, Kozo Kitahara, learned the trade from his father and continues it in his old studio. He is one of the fifteen who are left in Japan. He has been making shakuhachi for twenty-five years, even though he is still young. He brings to his work a sense of humbleness and dedication which is immediately communicated. Loving the bamboo itself, he cannot even bring himself to eat its shoots. In the winter, he goes up alone into the mountains, where he selects each one of the stems he will work. To stand thus in silence in the snow of a bamboo grove is his only holiday. The bamboo dries for three months on the roof of his house and then seasons in the dark for three years before its condition is ideal. During this season-

ing process the stems are trimmed into rough lengths, leaving a portion of flaring root at the base of each, which will become the bell end of the finished instrument.

When large sculptural forms began to appear, the attitude about looms changed. No longer was the loom seen as a tool which made the production of cloth faster and simpler. The loom suddenly was considered old-fashioned, a relic of the past to be disposed of quickly, so that textiles could be considered up to date and in step with the 20th century. Weaving seemed dreary and time consuming, while the newly celebrated off-hand glass blowing looked so effortless, almost magical. It was the time of the "happening" and the light show. Conceptual art and on-site installations began to appear.

The loom can most easily produce cloth of a rectangular shape. There also is a limited range of yarn sizes which it can handle comfortably. The new kind of work required expansion in many directions, shape among them. Explorations of off-loom processes began. It didn't seem to matter that twining, plaiting, netting, bobbin lace, and the myriad of techniques done without benefit of a loom were in fact more time consuming—they didn't *look* that way. Basketry was a direct outgrowth of this attitude. Interest in off-loom techniques for textile construction soon faded as artists moved on to felt and handmade paper. Only in basketry did that interest continue with vigor. The unrestricted shapes, materials, and techniques were focused by the notion of the vessel form. Here were individual three-dimensional forms which made use of the off-loom techniques and which had no need for elaborate hanging devices or armatures.

It is surprising how few substantial books have been written about baskets. There have always been how-to books, but rarely have there been books that deal seriously with the other aspects of basketry. Otis Tufton Mason's *Aboriginal American Basketry*, published in 1902, is an exception, though the book's publication was as much due to an interest in native Americans as to an interest in their baskets. Another exception is Bignia Kuoni's very fine book, *Cesteria tradicional iberica*, written in Spanish and published in 1981. It is an attempt to record the basketry traditions of Spain and Portugal while the traditions are still alive. I find myself wondering how much time will have to pass before the people who now make strictly utilitarian baskets will begin to make the art baskets which are now being made in this country. Will any of us, the contemporary American basketmakers, ever again make those useful baskets related to crops and harvesting?

I once had a Chinese-American student who was interested in doing research on traditional Chinese baskets (and there *is* a long tradition). She could read Chinese, so she was able to search the East Asian Library as well as the local university library. No luck. She finally located one book on the subject, written by a prominent Western anthropologist. There were a few photographs, and a short text which said in effect that there is nothing written on Chinese baskets. Chinese scholars apparently did not find baskets a worthy subject for books, no matter how important they are in ordinary life, or perhaps *because* they are omnipresent in ordinary life.

One really important influence on contemporary basketmaking has been the idea of the package. That concept covers a wide range, from packaging and presentation in advertising to the great wrapped sculptures of Christo. The exhibition, The Package, shown in 1959 at the Museum of Modern Art in New York, anticipated the interest in the vessel form. Books followed: *How to Wrap Five Eggs*, *How to Wrap Five More Eggs*, and *Tsutsumi*. The 1975 exhibition, The Art of the Japanese Package, was the first exhibit of Japanese packaging to appear outside Japan. It captivated a wide audience, including the textile world. Though the artists who currently are making baskets don't consider baskets packaging or advertising, we all present our thoughts on inside and outside space through our own finite personal bundles.

The question of labeling is always with us. A strange phenomenon has occurred in a number of exhibits in the last few years, most notably in a well-advertised exhibit, Intimate Architecture, at MIT. Clothing is described as architecture, textiles are described as painting, baskets as sculpture. There seems to be an attempt to make textiles or baskets more important. I don't think it works. The only people who pay attention to it are the textile people, or the basketmakers, and they already know that textiles and baskets are important.

In the spring of 1986 Lawrence Dawson, Senior Museum Anthropologist at the Lowie Museum of Anthropology, University of California, Berkeley, gave a lecture on the migration of basketry techniques and styles in prehistoric times from northern Asia to the north coast of the United States. One of the particularly interesting aspects of Dawson's lecture was a description of the types of prehistoric baskets which traveled. Twined baskets, such as fishing and berry baskets, had a tradition which remained unchanged in the new land as long as the specific need for which they were made continued to exist. Coiling, however, was a somewhat later technique, perhaps invented in North America. It spread in areas where twining traditions had long been entrenched, and it wasn't bound by the time-honored rules and regulations which governed twining. As Dawson stated:

> In areas where coiling spread in later times it was always received by the local people as a foreign idea, and therefore unencumbered by rules, whereas their traditional basketry was governed by nearly inflexible rules of manufacture and decoration. When coiling became known from neighbors or by trade it was welcomed as a novel technique in which one could freely extemporize and innovate.

In southern California designs were sometimes translated intact from twined baskets to coiled baskets with one important change: two stitches were used in coiling for every stitch in twining. If, however, the design was not taken directly from twining, there were no restrictions at all on the design. Therefore, coiling was much freer than the other techniques. Today's situation seems similar: ignorance of the traditional restrictions on design and technique leaves the contemporary basketmaker free to experiment with everything—materials, technique, color, scale.

It's curious to note that while basketmakers are now looking for firm, self-supporting materials, jewelers have begun to explore the use of textile techniques with wire. Generally, they have been attempting to construct precious and miniature basketry structures as body ornament. Potters, too, have taken to the basket form. The baskets of clay or metal make us aware of the essence of baskets. They emphasize the pliability, surface treatments, and complex structural variations possible in the more usual basketry materials. Seeing the "hard" baskets makes us see the softer ones, just as Oldenburg's soft typewriter makes us see all typewriters in a new way.

It is not the materials used which make contemporary baskets valu-

Scaffolding constructed from
bamboo. Photo: Dana Levy from
**Bamboo** (John Weatherhill, Inc.:
Tokyo, Japan).

able. This quote from *Bamboo* describes traditional art, yet it also seems to refer to contemporary baskets.

> The crafts of bamboo are very pure. This is because bamboo itself as a raw material has almost no financial value. Thus the estimation set on those articles made by masters of the traditional crafts derives entirely from the skill and art of their hands. It is the craftsmanship itself which is prized. . . . This is more true since bamboo is not by its nature a material which can be expected to last a long time.

One of the interesting features of the contemporary basketry movement is that it is almost exclusively a North American phenomenon. Its growth so far has been associated with art schools and textile departments at universities, or with textile exhibits at galleries and museums. There does not appear to be much of a parallel development outside this continent. Baskets obviously are being made elsewhere, but as part of an older tradition, not as part of this same movement. In 1981 an exhibit called Vannerie Traditionnelle d'Afrique et d'Asie et Nouvelle Vannerie was held in Lausanne. All the basketmakers represented in the small contemporary section were from the United States. The same was true of the exhibit Fibres Art 85, at the Musee des Arts Decoratifs in Paris.

There are signs of the "new" basket forms being made elsewhere. The catalog of a 1982 traveling exhibit in Japan, Art and/or Craft: USA and Japan, showed a few. In the summer of 1985 I met a student in Sweden who was interested in investigating non-traditional basket forms. She was encouraged by friends and teachers to come to the U.S. to study, since the audience here would be more receptive to her work. In England, judging from the magazine *Crafts*, there is also the beginning of interest in new basketry.

The interest in new basketry in this country seems to have originated mainly on the coasts, primarily in California. Perhaps this is because the coasts are most affected by trade and new ideas. It might be the adventurous spirit associated with the West, or it might simply be the influence of Ed Rossbach on his students.

In the art of the 20th century, there has been a break with tradition. New materials, new methods, new ideas are embraced. The new baskets, too, break with traditional basketry. If there is any relation to older work it is that the new baskets seem related to bridges and scaffolding in non-industrialized countries, rather than to the baskets of those countries.

Baskets. Even the word seems humble, self-effacing, and traditional. Some people have asked why I refer to my works as baskets when they aren't the traditional useful baskets. No one expects a concert of contemporary music to sound like Bach, or a contemporary painting to look like a Leonardo. Strange, then, that many expect contemporary baskets to be just like baskets of another century.

This attitude is not unique to the public, either. Critics and writers also suffer from a time lag. I once heard a thoughtful talk on basketry presented at the opening of an exhibition of contemporary baskets. The speaker called for an appreciation of contemporary baskets by describing the beauty of natural materials and traditional techniques as they continue in the new work. As admirable as the traditional baskets may be, following in that tradition is not the aim of most artists making baskets today. Not one piece in the above mentioned show was a traditionally constructed basket made of natural materials.

The new movement in basketry seems to have practitioners all over this country. There is a wonderful diversity among us, perhaps because of the solitary nature of the work. Most of the new basketmakers have had art training, but are self-taught in the skills of basketmaking. Just a few years ago there was no category in fiber shows for basketmakers. Now they are publishing books about us!

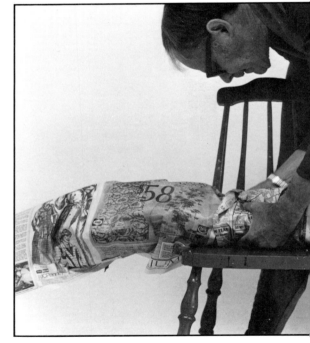

# ED ROSSBACH

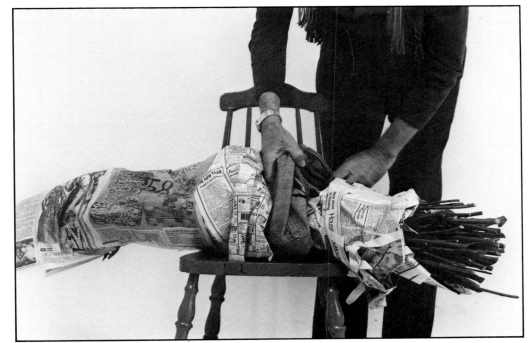

Our house is full of baskets. They're stored everywhere in the place. They're in clothes closets, kitchen cupboards, cedar chests, and, mostly, in cardboard cartons. I am obsessed with them; they are oppressive, and yet my wife and I keep buying more, and I keep making more. They seldom depart the premises once they get inside, and if they do,

Below: Untitled, newspaper and plastic, 10"x10", 1976.
Top right: Untitled, willow with raw hide, 8"x10", 1968.
Bottom right: Untitled, corn husk, 9"x12", 1969.

for an exhibition, they almost always return to find their places have been taken by other baskets. But they must be taken in. They are like the sentimental characters in a poem by Robert Frost.

I hate to part with baskets that I've spent time with. Someone—someone I don't even know—sent me an everyday basket (everyday, at least, to the people where it was made) and said that when I had lived with it for a while I should pass it along to someone else. I can't do it.

My own baskets—those that I have made—are kept in places where I need not look at them for any length of time. They are more satisfying when I see them only occasionally. I've heard that some people feel that way about their children. Once in awhile I'll take one of my baskets out of storage and look at it for about ten minutes. Usually that's enough. Sometimes the basket seems better than I remember it, sometimes it seems worse. I know within ten minutes. Memory, for me, is not a reliable tool of judging baskets; I have to confront the basket itself. Sometimes there are baskets I have

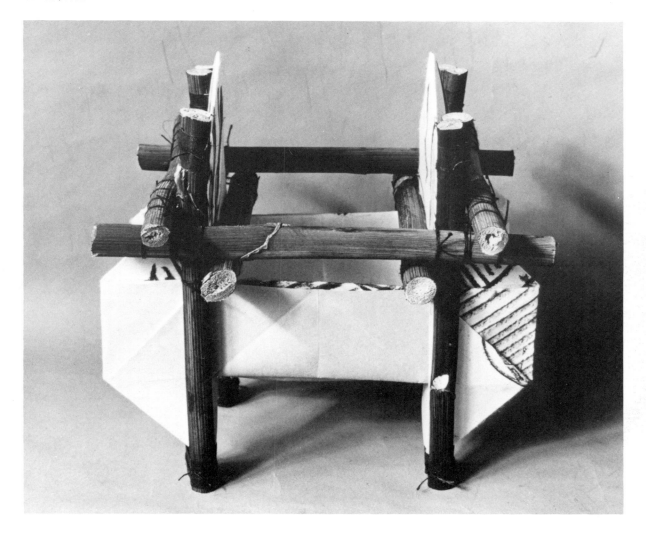

made that I have completely forgotten. I realize that if they hadn't turned up by chance, I never would have thought of them again. They are like so many incidents in travel, never consciously thought of again.

The strange thing is that I'm not anxious to sell my baskets, or to give them away. If I really like a basket that I have made, even though I almost never look at it, I want to keep it. If I don't like it, I don't want to sell it, either. If I do sell a good basket I say, "That was a good basket. It has gone out of my life forever. I won't even be able to remember it. I probably shouldn't have sold it."

I guess what I am trying to say in this roundabout fashion is that baskets mean a great deal to me. I have a couple of Indian baskets from the Puget Sound area that keep speaking to me. They're around all the time. I never get tired of them. I also have some little plaited things from Indonesia made for tourists. I never get tired of them either. All these baskets seem so remarkable, I'm amazed that everyone isn't astonished—struck dumb—by their wonder.

19

# JAN BUCKMAN

When stories and legends are lost, culture dies. The baskets I make are legends growing out of the collective memories of my heritage. They speak of a culture, of honor, of commitment, of magic, of spirituality. They reflect a time when art and religion were fused with the demands of daily survival, a time when the sacredness of every object and every action was crucial to the blessings of that survival. My baskets express my effort to emulate these qualities in my own life.

My work comes from the contrast between what is, and what was; what is, and what can be. The following are some of the contrasts I attend to:

. . . watched a healthy young man on a riding lawn mower, plugged into a Walkman, mowing a postage-stamp-sized lawn. . . .

*It took Datsolalee, a Washo Indian, one full year to complete a basket.*

. . . stood in awe in a gourmet food store at the array of electric potato peelers, microwave merry-go-rounds complete with

Untitled, waxed linen, 3¾"x5½", 1985. Photo: Peter Lee.

painted horses, food processors that do everything but swallow the food for you . . .

*My 75-year-old neighbor handed me a small maple branch that blew down in yesterday's wind, telling me it will boil a good cup of "coffee" on the cookstove.*

. . . walked by the Hollywood Video store and stopped to watch a man and boy filling a grocery cart with movies for the weekend. I wonder what you might see in their eyes Sunday night. (And now I hear you can have videos delivered to your door) . . .

*There was a man who dug himself a pond over a period of many years. As part of his daily walk, he carried away two buckets of dirt.*

. . . there are elevators that express their desire that you have a nice day in the two dimensional voice of a computer. At least you don't have to come up with a Christmas gift to give this operator . . .

*We should, I have read, ask forgiveness of the trees and plants as we harvest them. Spent a day cutting ironwood saplings to weave a trellis. Asked for a lot of blessings*

Left: Untitled work in
progress, waxed linen.
Photo: Peter Lee.
**Above left:** Detail of
untitled, waxed linen,
4½"x5⅜", 1982. Photo:
Jim Christoffersen.
Photo of Jan Buckman by
Thomas Paul.

*and felt rather foolish talking to the trees, yet as I sit in their shade, making a basket, I sense a presence.*

. . . for people who have trouble keeping track of their lives and possessions, there is a keychain that reveals its location by playing Beethoven's Ninth Symphony . . .

*My neighbor announced to me that it was one year ago today that my son helped tear down her old corn crib. She was freezing peas. As she reuses each plastic lid, she adds another piece of masking tape, recording not only the date, but some significant event or vision of the day. The sun rose red that morning.*

. . . heard of a man who spent a full year inside the Water Tower in Chicago and never had to leave the building. He was fed, entertained, supplied, cooled, heated, all within the confines of two city blocks. The only sunshine came through tinted windows. Wonder what finally made him open the door to the outside . . .

*An Indian woman, after drying berries, tanning deer hides, digging roots, gathering firewood, sits down to work on a basket to be used for storing nuts. She feels the need to make this one precious, and twines the image of blackbirds as they fly through the now-leafless trees.*

I am often asked how I can spend 70 hours making a basket. My answer is: How can people rush through their days in order to spend 70 hours of their time watching television? I try to make baskets an integral part of my life, in context and in harmony with the things I do every day, not something separate which demands a solitary space, behind the closed doors of an austere white-walled studio. Weeding the garden, splitting wood, and baking bread are not tasks that I must hurry to complete in order to return to a basket. The daily duties of my life feed my basketmaking and basketmaking nourishes my living. I am learning to honor time; not with a sense of urgency or pressure but through a respect for details.

I take pleasure in the process of making a basket, of persisting until it becomes precious. Beyond this, the baskets must speak for themselves. The imag-

ery on the pieces is not more or less than my curiosity and response to my environment. One could see horizons, or the silhouette of a scrub oak which has survived countless storms perched on a rocky cliff, or the trail and wanderings of seen and unseen beings on the forest floor.

Left: Untitled, waxed linen, 4¼"x7", 1985.
Below: Untitled, waxed linen, 4½"x3¾", 1984.
Photos: Peter Lee.

Left: Untitled, waxed linen, 5⅞"x4½", 1983. Photo: Jim Christoffersen.
Below left: Untitled, waxed linen, 4½"x3¾", 1984. Photo: Peter Lee.
Below right: Untitled, waxed linen, 4"x5", 1985. Photo: Peter Lee.
Opposite: Untitled, waxed linen, 4⅜"x4", 1986. Photo: Peter Lee.

25

# JANE SAUER

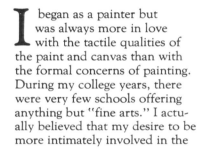

"Polychrome III," waxed linen, paint, 4½"x10", 1985. Photo: Matthew Taylor.
Photo of Jane Sauer by Red Elf.

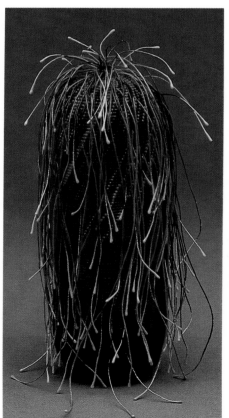

I began as a painter but was always more in love with the tactile qualities of the paint and canvas than with the formal concerns of painting. During my college years, there were very few schools offering anything but "fine arts." I actually believed that my desire to be more intimately involved in the artistic process was a negative regression to "women's handiwork," and that the only *real* artists were painters and sculptors. My work with textiles began in 1975 after I matured in my own thinking, thanks to the education given me by my children and the women's movement. I also was temporarily unable to paint at that time because of a back injury. After trying loom weaving, rug hooking, direct dyeing on fabric, and needlepoint, I found basketry and since then have not thought of doing anything else. I must admit that I am obsessive about my art form.

Because I have a husband, children, various animals, and the problems and responsibilities that surround us all, I am constantly involved in an inner struggle, or maybe I should say *war*, wanting to do my art work and wanting to take care of the rest of my life. I try to work at least eight hours each weekday and some over the weekend. When I am close to a deadline I do nothing and think nothing but art for several days or maybe even weeks. My family is very supportive, and I am not

26

"Nest/Nested/Nestle,"
waxed linen, silk, feathers,
4"x6", 1980.
Inset: "Ceremonial Basket,"
waxed linen, silk,
3½"x5½", 1979. Photos:
Huntley Barad.

expected to make dinner, clean house, or wash clothes. I think women my age (48) find it very difficult not to perform domestic duties naturally, because we were taught that this is our burden. I have had to train myself to share household responsibility with the rest of the family, so some of my struggle is within myself.

My studio is a converted unattached garage. I like being able to work where I can still have contact with my children. My eleven-year-old has a shelf for her own art supplies in my studio. My other children, who enjoyed doing art work when they were younger, check in occasionally. My husband frequently works in my studio also. The space seems at times to be very private and personal, and at times it is the center of our family life.

My art work is the container for the tensions of my life. I firmly believe in the power of a well-designed, beautifully executed basket, but I want to go beyond that. I am always saying something in my work, searching for forms that are archetypal. I find the struggle to go beyond is accompanied by fear of failing,

Opposite: "Earth Vessels," waxed linen, paint, 3"x6" and 5"x8", 1982. Photo: Huntley Barad.
Below left: "No Exit," waxed linen, paint, silk, 2"x18", 1985. Photo: Matthew Taylor.
Center: "Breaking Old Patterns," raw linen, waxed linen, 3¼"x10¼", 1984. Photo: Matthew Taylor.
Right: "Color Factor," raw linen, waxed linen, 3½"x10", 1984. Photo: Matthew Taylor.

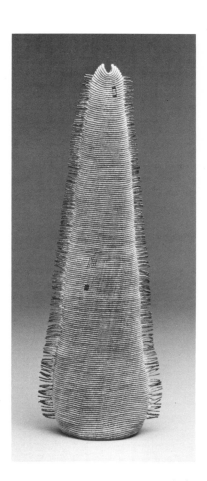

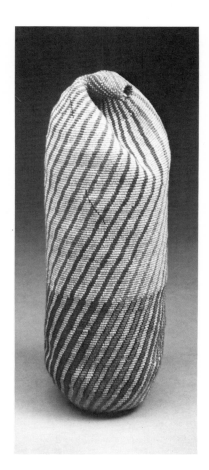

anxiety over wasting time and materials to create a failure, and concern that I am not pushing the boundaries far enough and fast enough. But at the same time there is the feeling of exhilaration during that magic time when things come together, when one idea is rushing toward another, when I am in new territory and have some control. I find agony and joy in searching to capture a sense of the unexpected, to reveal the magic of form, to bring order to chaos, to bring together the mind and the spirit. I hope to make forms that have a universal emotional impact, that are generic, yet are allegorical to my own life. My shapes have become progressively simpler, and I have become more involved with their messages. I have been using symbols to express circumstances, tensions, contradictions, and the interplay of relationships in my life.

My newest forms are directly related to a recent trip to Japan. The Eastern experience further deepened my resolve to "simplify and intensify." The Japanese have a wonderful way of isolating and simplifying an object so as to make it become more

important. Japanese art revealed visual language, a high regard for craftsmanship, and the stretch for perfection, coupled with mysterious, serene, meditative qualities.

Because I am making both baskets and sculpture I am con-

cerned with structure. The process of knotting, the technique I am now using exclusively, is a slow procedure of building a structure row upon row. I have chosen to develop the possibilities of this one process instead of exploring a number of different

methods of building with threads. I enjoy the rhythm of the process, and there still are many new techniques to try. Knotting creates a grid and therefore almost begs to become a pattern.

Man's constant desire to make stripes and patterns is

Left, from left: "Entrance with No Exit," waxed linen, paint, 6½"x18", "Soft Daggers," waxed linen, paint, 4½"x10", "Subliminal Messages," waxed linen, paint, 2"x19", 1985-86. Photo: Red Elf.

Below: "Adolescent Fascination," waxed linen, dyed silk, 3¼"x10", 1984. Photo: Matthew Taylor. Opposite: "Celebration," waxed linen, paint, 4½"x7½", 1985. Photo: Matthew Taylor.

fascinating. Besides making baskets, every culture has made stripes and patterns. I share this same attraction and desire to decorate obsessively, and frequently I need to let this desire dominate my art. Patterns and stripes, of course, require the added dimension of color. I love the challenge of discovering what I can make color do. How can I make you *feel* by the color and shape I use? How can I make one color into several colors by varying the quantity and by changing the color's surroundings? I have begun to experiment with painting on threads so I can have all the colors I want, not just those available commercially. I feel as if I have come full circle; I am using the painting skills that I began with.

I am still awed by the fact that, without using any tools or technical equipment, but by just moving my fingers, I can make this object called a basket. I can make a sculptural form with patterns, stripes, grids, shape, symbols, gentle stain of the fibers, vibrant or pungent colors, and I have only just begun my exploration of the endless possibilities.

# KARI LØNNING

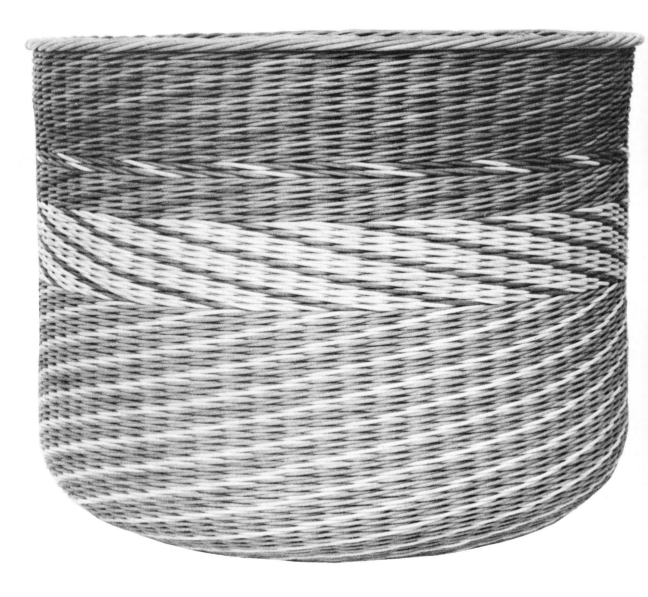

**M**y interest in basketry began as an intrigue with construction. For my first basket, I used a copper wire tea strainer as my model. The woven wire held its shape and created a pattern of its own. Soon after, I took a basketry workshop. In the beginning, I made baskets for the fun of it— the process was so time consuming, I couldn't imagine doing it for a living. But within a few weeks, I was doing little else.

I always work in dyed or natural rattan. It is completely controllable, and has little character of its own. It allows me to weave the "thrown" forms which I was incapable of mastering as a potter. By using fiber-reactive dyes instead of glazes, I can achieve an infinite spectrum which I can count on reproducing. Since most of the work I do is by special order, this is a very important factor. At present, I am working with a muted palette of pale pink, lavender, gray, blue and green. With my production pieces, I know what each basket will look like before I begin it. In the other work, I hold a vague idea as to general form or color but, so far, no piece was completed as it was first conceived.

Many people still feel they have to put something into a basket to justify its existence. Although my production work is constructed to withstand use, its primary purpose is not its function. The essence of baskets, as containers, is still very important to me, but my reason for making baskets rather than working in another medium is that baskets are the most appropriate vehicle through which I can experiment with color, design and form. The double-walled pieces are constructed so that they *already* contain something—space. For me, they are an affirmation of what baskets can be.

My favorite place to work is on my front porch. It faces south, so even when it's cold, I can be in the sun, protected from the north winds. The porch is surrounded by flowering trees, bushes, and perennials, which bloom as soon as the ground thaws and last late into fall. Colors, scents and textures abound. When it does get too cold to be outside, I move into a studio off my kitchen. There, too, I am surrounded by flowering plants and bulbs and greenery. Though I have a room piled high with assorted dye lots of

reed, baskets in progress or finished, office materials and slides
and photographs, I can't have
clutter around me while I work.
Even having the wrong music on
while I work is distracting.

I am now working with more
decorators, and have been trying
to balance the colors I want with
the colors they want. A subtle
change toward more muted and
gray tones seems to have satisfied us all. As the baskets got
larger, I put more energy into
using contemporary colors. The
production pieces moved away
from the craft market into the
home furnishings market. Here it
seems people can see the baskets
first as design statements and
then decide whether they are
interested in them as baskets.

It's hard to make the shift
from a production frame of
mind to a more abstract, allow-
it-to-come way of thinking. I
don't know what my work will
be like in the future; there are
still many possibilities I want to
explore. I may not even be working in basketry, but I will be
making or designing something,
and I will be addressing the fascination I have with space and
color.

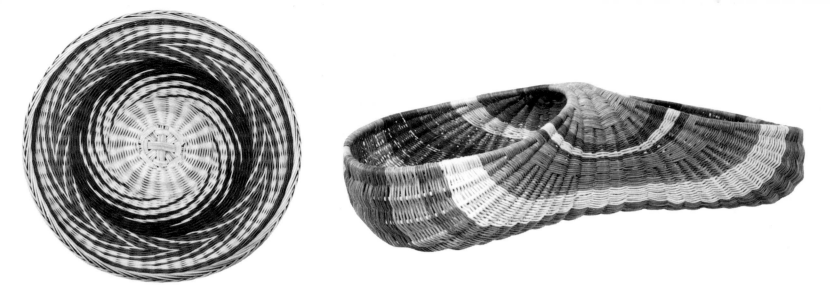

Photo of basket grouping at left courtesy Meredith Gallery, Baltimore, Maryland.

I am a basketmaker. I work with metallic fiber, and glean industrial metals from alleys behind machine shops. This started several years ago, when one day I passed a machine shop and saw long, thin strips of iridescent blue and purple steel turnings in the trash bin. Then I discovered the recycling center where I used to hunt for just the right tin cans to snip and paint. Later I found that the trash bins at the farm implement store contained the most wonderful tractor gears. I would pile them up and paint them with transparent paint.

When I started to work in fibers I always tried to integrate metal turnings with the natural wool and linens as I used the processes of weaving, felting, and basketry. I had always thought of the turnings as fiber, and found I could use them in much the same way as any other fiber. First I made a basket of mostly natural fiber with just a little metal. Then the baskets became mostly metal, sometimes with a bit of natural material like date fruit stalks, banana bark, or mink.

I use industrial metals like

# KAREN S. TURNIDGE

copper, stainless steel, brass, aluminum, tin, and other metals. I go to local machine shops and gather curling metal chips as they come rolling off the lathes. I search through trash barrels to find the particular turning I need. Lately I have been working with a machinist who has helped me develop turnings to use for specific purposes, because I could no longer find enough of the same kind of shavings in the trash. I also work with woven wire, and wire that I find.

I try to work with as many basketry techniques as possible and add to them metal techniques that enhance my basketry. I have found the unique characteristics of metal to be a challenge and a help in making baskets. Through experimentation I discovered metal could be used like vines or twigs in traditional basketry techniques like twining, plaiting, or coiling. The turnings are so flexible I can knit, crochet, or "felt" with them. I have knit both with wire and turnings, and have used crochet or looping as well. Felting, as I think of it, refers to the fiber technique in which wool fibers are meshed together using

heated water and pressure. The same technique can be used with turnings of a special shape.

Some of my plaited baskets and pulled warp baskets have the see-through qualities of woven metal. Metal can also be squishy and soft, as in my plaited tin baskets and some crocheted baskets. I like the contrast of soft and hard, and the visually similar characteristics of the linear wire, woven wire and spikey gleam of mink.

Opposite: "Fire Series: Kindle," copper, wire, 7"x17", 1985. Above: "Bristle," copper, wire, computer-aided design, 13"x8", 1984. Photos: Suzanne Coles-Ketcham. Photo of Karen Turnidge by Darrell Turnidge.

I treat the metal fiber in various ways before making it into baskets. Sometimes I pound on it with a hammer, or bend it, or rivet it, but mostly I enjoy baking it. I touch it with a torch, or use a kiln to color one strand at a time. If I'm really feeling brave, I bake the whole basket at once. I use heat coloring with stainless steel to bring out golds, purples, and blues (my cool palette). When heat is applied to copper, reds, oranges, pinks, and silvers are produced. Aluminum and titanium can be anodized for color, a process that I am now starting to use. By using impressionistic color and constructions that indicate action, I try to convey liveliness, energy, and celebration.

In 1983 I was introduced to the technique of pulled warp basketry and I have used computer graphics with a homemade program to design baskets to be made with this technique. Basically, a view of one edge of the basket is drawn, then the whole basket appears on the screen, then a pattern can be printed for weaving—all in a matter of minutes. I have also done some experiments with a computer

photographic process to make graphics for use with loom-woven baskets.

When planning a basket I think mostly of the material I have on hand, because that determines the size, color, and technique I will use. My drawings and sketches for my work are usually many variations of form, and rarely have I completely followed my drawing as I work. I have been inspired by the ancient and contemporary clay pottery that I have studied, and modeling with clay is a way to sketch ideas for baskets. Shapes can be formed with it very quickly. One of my small baskets was made in much the same way as a clay pot. I just pinched the copper to shape and added knitted copper as structural support on the outside.

In my studies of metal techniques I have gained endless inspiration from metalsmiths and jewelers and the richness of their ideas, their sculptural design, and their fine craftsmanship.

I am a basketmaker because I love the basket's symbolism. It reminds me of man's first action of gathering food and of the first temporary baskets. I like to push the symbol into the present by thinking of contemporary themes, like nutrition. The double helix construction has inspired some of my baskets. In my mind it symbolizes new life, as in the DNA molecule. The cell wall also gives inspiration for baskets. Various energy sources inspire my work: the sun, wave action, swirling water, and fire. As I work I think of solar energy and the power of energy in water. I think of light or of a hearth fire. The feminine symbolism of basketry for me as a mother is involved with the nurturing and protecting of life. The process of going round and round as one makes a coiled basket makes me think of the recycling of industrial metals. As a basketmaker I enjoy bringing the elements of metal, fiber, and names together to convey the symbolism of ideas that interest me.

My last name is Turnidge (Turn-edge), which originated in England and referred to a lathe worker. I never really thought about it much when I was developing my ideas, but the name is appropriate.

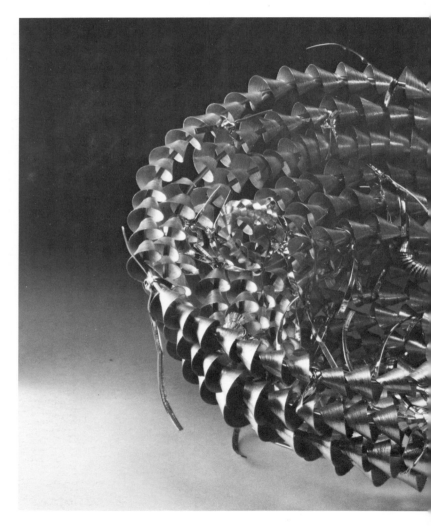

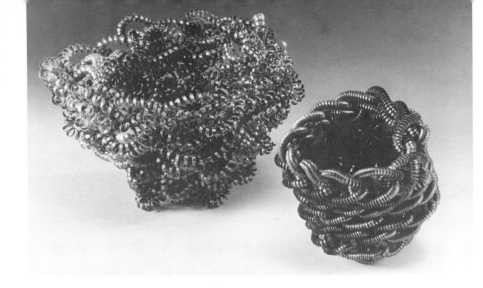

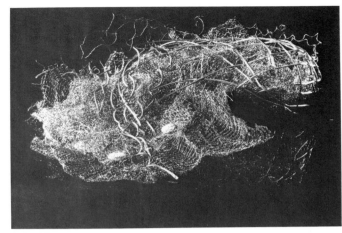

Clockwise, from above left:
"Crochet Olé," stainless
steel, 5"x8", 1984.
"Crochet Cup," stainless
steel, 3"x4", 1984.
"Catching Agate Tides,"
copper, 16"x9", 1985.
"Jittery (All Tied up in
Knots)," brass, stainless
steel, 13"x5", 1985. "Party
Pizza, No Anchovies,"
copper, 14"x4", 1984.
"Aluminating," aluminum,
12"x9", 1985. Photos:
Suzanne Coles-Ketcham.

# PATTI LECHMAN

I can't remember when I wasn't involved with fiber—it's always been a part of my life. I sewed by hand as a child, dressing dolls. By the time I was twelve, I was making a lot of my own clothes. My mother, sister and I developed the skill of copying garments when my sister and I were in college and wanted more "label" clothes than the family budget allowed. My mother taught me to knit, and we turned out intricate cable-patterned sweaters with tiny crocheted egg-shaped buttons.

An interest in art came early, too. My father loved to sketch and draw, and there were always books around, books on drawing the figure, lettering, drawing trees. When I was seven, he gave me an oil paint set, a beautiful wooden box filled with shiny little tubes of paint, small bottles of turpentine and linseed oil, brushes, and a palette. I began painting immediately, and "sold" my first painting to a school friend in exchange for a real coconut she had brought back from a family trip to Florida.

My interest in textiles and art continued through high school. In college I worked toward a degree in home economics. I took art courses as electives, but had little time to do any exploring. After graduation, I spent three years working on a Master of Fine Arts degree in ceramics, and kept trying to do clay and fiber pieces that worked together. They never really succeeded. A jewelry instructor with whom I did independent study said, "Patti, I don't know

Right: Work in progress. Photo of Patti Lechman by Bert Sharpe.

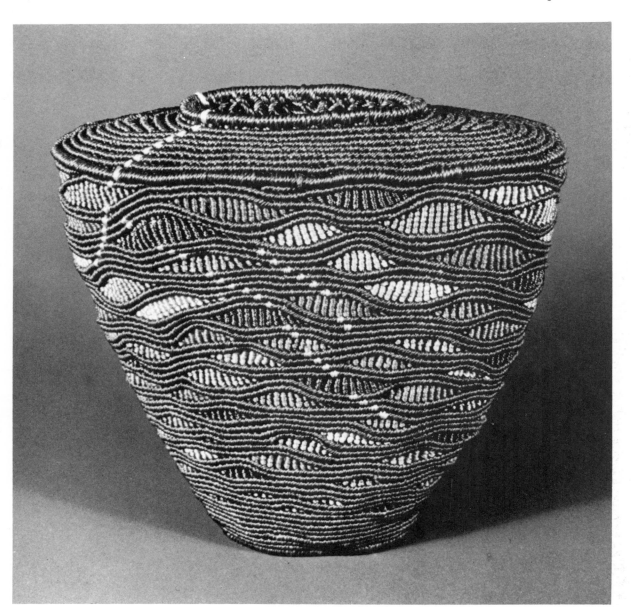

why you have to do those clay and fiber things. The fiber alone is so much better!" She was right and I knew it.

After finishing my M.F.A., I moved to Memphis, Tennessee, and taught art appreciation and ceramics at the community college. Having my hands in the clay all day at school made me crave working in fibers again. A happy accident pushed me back into fiber work and basketry. I decided to go to Penland for a summer session, but sent my registration too late to get into the clay course I wanted. My second choice was a class in fiber, and I worked 12 to 16 hours a day on baskets during the two weeks I spent there. The work was ideal for me because it was portable, clean, and I could work on the pieces even when I was physically tired from teaching. For several years I didn't have a studio space at home where I could do clay. Fiber was much easier to deal with.

Two summers later I went to a workshop that dealt with color and design on small scale knotted work. I wanted to use color more in my work, and from the first I loved working on a very

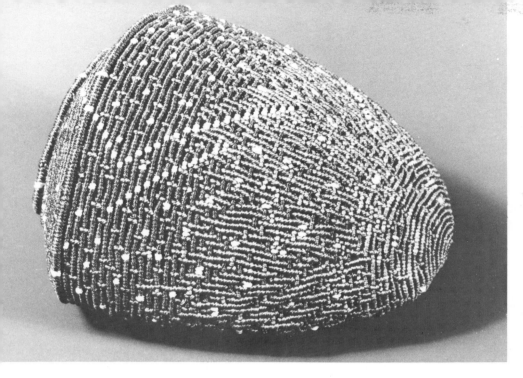

small scale. Everything about the new approach began to work for me. I experimented with various materials before settling on the lightly sized nylon that I use. It has a crispness that I couldn't find in linen, cotton, or silk though I liked the idea of those fibers. I take some comfort now, however, in knowing that the flag on the moon is made of nylon and should last forever. (After having problems with moths in wool, I appreciate that quality.) I just couldn't make the natural fibers do what I wanted them to do. I dye some of my colors because the yarn I use isn't available in a wide spectrum. When the pieces are completed, I treat them with a color preservative and thread sealer, so I'm satisfied about colorfastness now.

Most of my pieces begin with styrofoam forms that I rasp or carve out of large blocks. I sit in the studio making a powdery mess as I file away at the styrofoam, creating several forms at a time. The pottery influence is apparent at this stage as I translate the vessel form of clay to the vessel container form in fiber.

I do most of my work (the

45

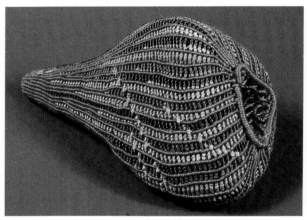

actual knot tying) at night while sitting with my knees pulled up, holding the work in place in front of me, close to eye level. The process is almost meditative for me; I untie myself as I tie knots in the pieces. I make baskets because I love them. I love the process and the product.

It all seems to be a logical culmination of years of experiences with fiber, with vessels, and with a quiet, contemplative way of working privately, a contrast to the draining physical work of the teaching which is my livelihood.

In writing artist's statements during the last few years I've

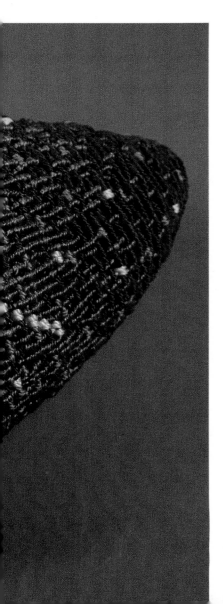

tried to be somewhat analytical about the pieces. What do they say? Are they really art? Does the fact that they are "pretty" make them trivial? We can't always know why something we do or see touches us, or speaks to us. Maybe all we know is that it does, or doesn't.

I want to do something visually delightful—a creation of grace and elegance, like a beautiful meal or a warm letter treasured by the recipient— something that makes a moment in time more beautiful, makes the spirit soar, maybe briefly, but joyfully. I also want to make art which doesn't reject the viewers, the participants, but envelops them with a warmth and doesn't require a level of understanding that only a mind educated in the aesthetics can respond to. I think I'm that way as a person. Maybe it has to do with "good manners." A friend once told me that I had "lovely" manners but that I was quite mysterious. I think the work has those qualities.

I do these baskets because I want to, because I love them, not to give other people pleasure but because they give *me* pleasure.

The traditional vessel is a functional form dealing with enclosure and access. While my vessels allude to function, they cannot be entered. I create structures that represent my thoughts and feelings about man's physical relationship to earth. As I look back to the late 1960's and early 1970's, I begin to understand how my work has evolved, and I can see a clear connection between the forms and the earth-rooted themes that have now emerged in my vessels. I now recognize that my work always concerned containment, protection and entrapment, and a particular curiosity about the passage from the known to the unknown.

In the late 1960's, I was making sculptural wall hangings and small stuffed fiber sculptures. I was searching for a technique that would enable me to use the fibers in a unique way; I was knitting, crocheting, embroidering, stuffing, beading, appliqueing and machine stitching, using these materials alone and sometimes combined. I leaned toward the three-dimensional and purely sculptural object. I experimented

Top: "Barren Vessel," fiber, rubber, acrylic, 8½"x10", 1985. Bottom: "Spirals," fiber, acrylic, straw, 6¼"x10½", 1985. Photos: Bob Hanson. Photo of Norma Minkowitz by Steve Minkowitz.

with fabric, using multilayer techniques such as reverse applique, which I taught and lectured on for a number of years.

The early 1970's were experimental years; I searched for ways of combining surface, structure, technique and content in a personal way. From that time to 1984 my work was divided between wearable and non-functional art. The female figure was common subject matter for both my wearables and sculptures, as were the box, egg, and ovoid shape.

From 1976 to 1978 I worked on a project which was a departure for me. I created a chair called "The Landscape of my Mind." I perceive it to be a combination of the functional art object and the purely non-functional object. The chair had a raised, linear quality inherent in knitting and crochet. It related the human form to the landscape. The body, when seated, would become one with the chair; the chair, which functioned as a container, was also a sculpture.

I did several non-functional boxes and a series of shoe forms that I feel were a bridge between

# NORMA MINKOWITZ

Right: "Connection II,"
fiber, acrylic, 8"x9", 1984.
Below: Detail of
"Connection II."
Opposite: "Hidden Places,"
fiber, acrylic, pencil,
hornet nest, 6"x10½",
1984. Photos: Bob Hanson.

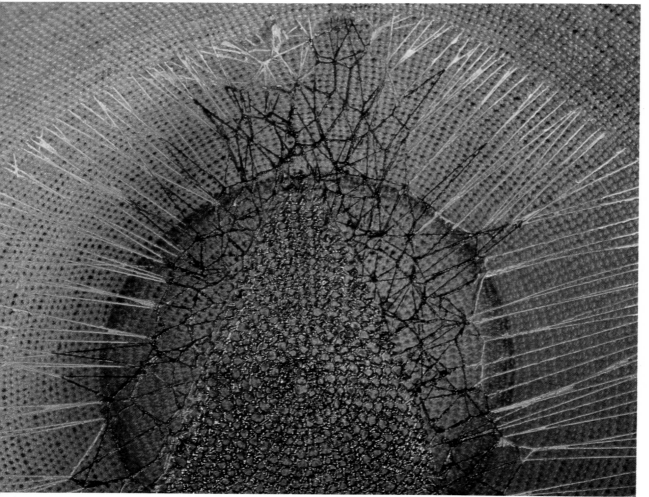

the wearables and containers. Shoes are also containers, but these shoes could not be worn; they were light, airy and incapable of holding any weight.

The new vessels have evolved and presently are my clearest form of expression. The structures of these "containers" also have gone through a transformation. At the beginning the vessels were more open, wide rims with narrow bottoms, expanding the idea of sky and air above and the bowels of the earth below. While some still retain that shape, they have become more closed, often cylindrical traps with no way in or out.

After years of stuffing, embroidering, crocheting, and knitting with solid closed forms, I have attained a method that best expresses my artistic goals in a way I feel is unique. My work is now open and delicate, but structural. This skeletal weightless quality is meant to express our fragile and vulnerable existence. My work continues to deal with containment, but in a new and exciting way. These vessels represent earth, they surround an inner space that alludes to function. The top is life, sky,

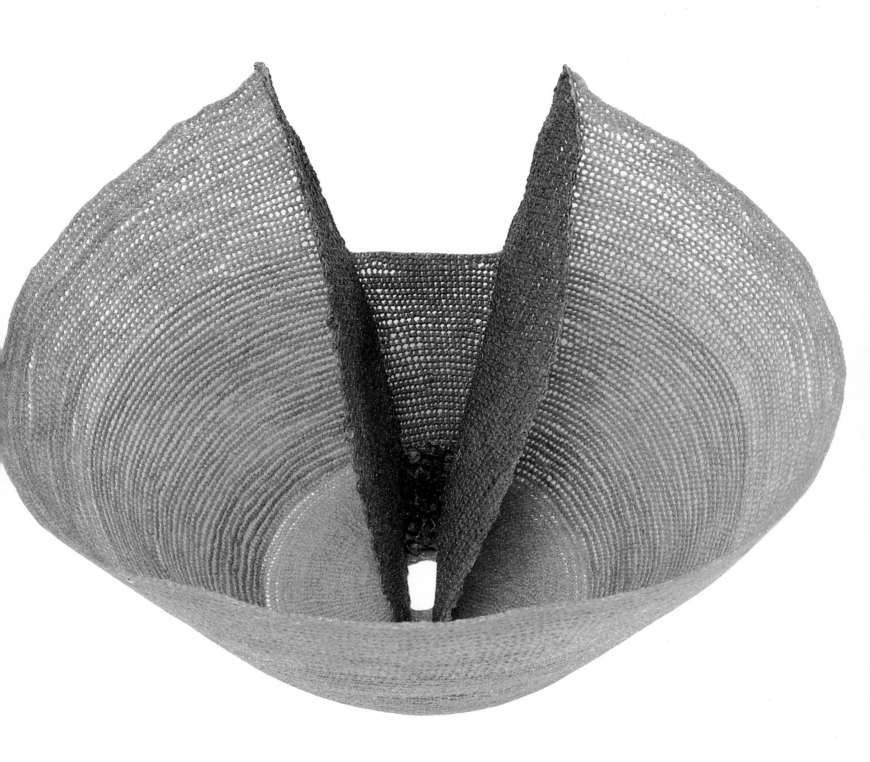

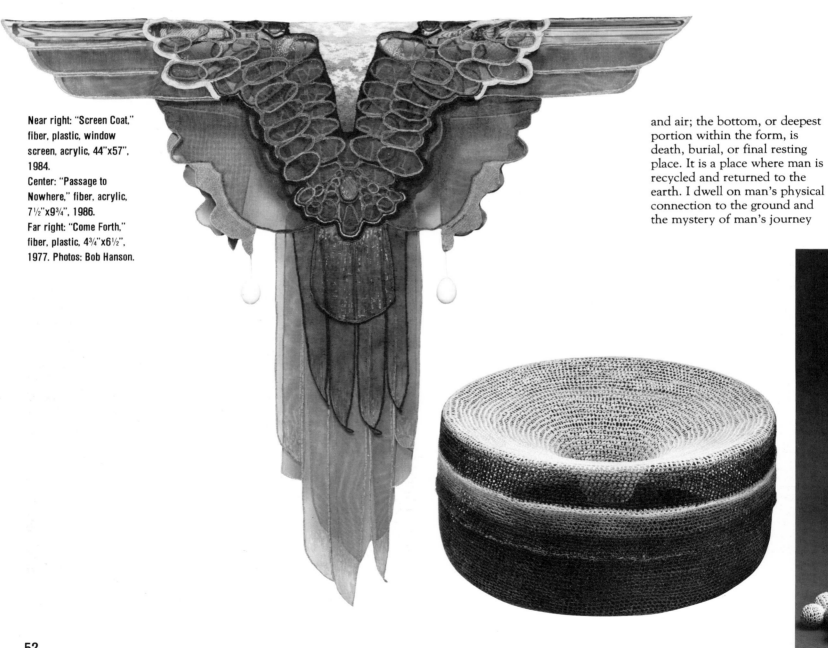

Near right: "Screen Coat," fiber, plastic, window screen, acrylic, 44"x57", 1984.
Center: "Passage to Nowhere," fiber, acrylic, 7½"x9¾", 1986.
Far right: "Come Forth," fiber, plastic, 4¾"x6½", 1977. Photos: Bob Hanson.

and air; the bottom, or deepest portion within the form, is death, burial, or final resting place. It is a place where man is recycled and returned to the earth. I dwell on man's physical connection to the ground and the mystery of man's journey from life to the unknown. My vessels address the lack of control one has over his destiny; a too-long life needing to end, or the premature end of one just beginning. This is the uncertainty and vulnerability I hope my work will communicate.

My artistic goal is to go beyond the structure and to impose meaning to my work. The choice of process has become part of the content. The quality of openness in combination with painting and drawing, and the utilization of earth-related found objects as well as man-made parts are just some of the personal additions.

Many of the new vessels are just of fiber, some are painted and drawn up with colored pencils, and some have different colors of threads creating patterns. I enjoy this play of materials, as it invites the viewer to dwell upon the illusion and perhaps not see any difference between paint and thread. For creating art, crochet is my primary technique; the flexible and organic qualities of fiber combined with the use of a single tool provide an intimate personal relationship with both the material and the object. I need to be responsible for, and have total control over, every aspect of the process and object in order to communicate my concepts, questions, and fantasies of man's physical and spiritual existence.

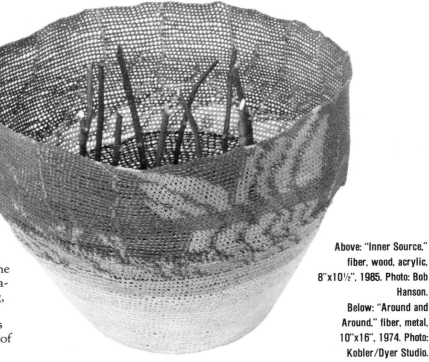

Above: "Inner Source," fiber, wood, acrylic, 8"x10½", 1985. Photo: Bob Hanson.
Below: "Around and Around," fiber, metal, 10"x16", 1974. Photo: Kobler/Dyer Studio.

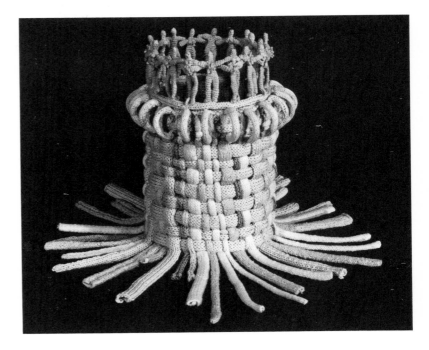

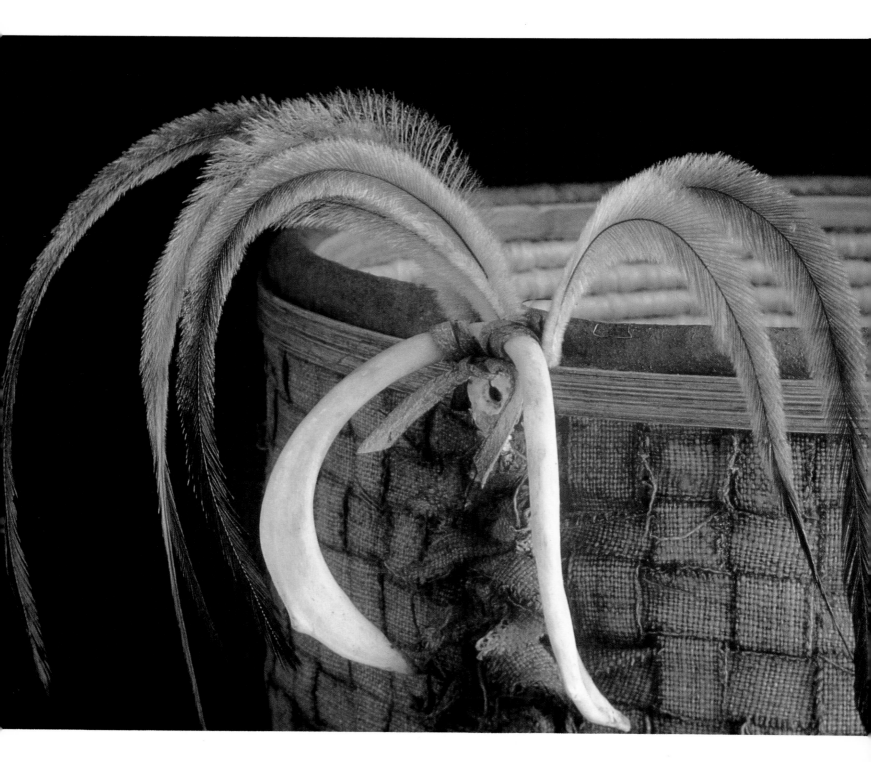

54

# LISSA HUNTER

Early morning is a lovely time in Maine. The sky over the Back Cove near my house is pink or orange or lavender or sometimes all three. As light overcomes dark I am usually trying to put things in order in my studio, sipping coffee, planning for the day by making a list. I like this time. The work table before me is covered with correspondence, work in progress, drawings, ledger sheets, the tools of the trade.

The day's activities may include making paper, coiling, answering letters, packing work, drawing, photographing work, stitching, or any number of seemingly unrelated tasks. The list is always longer than the day accommodates and so the leftovers will go on the next day's list.

One of the pleasant things about being a basketmaker is the sheer beauty and friendliness of the materials. No metal shavings or anvils or motorized saws or turpentine odors or clay dust to live with. This is particularly important when your studio is an integral part of your home, as is mine. The living room has been given over to studio space.

An 8-by-8-foot section of wallboard is used for drawing and collage assembly. Work tables and shelves house jars of beads, spools of thread, paints, brushes, fabric yardage, books, feathers, leather. Spindles with raffia, splint, sweet grass and iris leaves hang over the west-facing window. All conspire to create an atmosphere of creative confusion and visual stimulation.

I like having visual juxtapositions and overlays around me all the time. Shelves and a bulletin board are covered with images

Opposite: Detail of "YooHoo Basket." Photo: Rob Karosis.
Photo of Lissa Hunter by Kirby Pilcher.

55

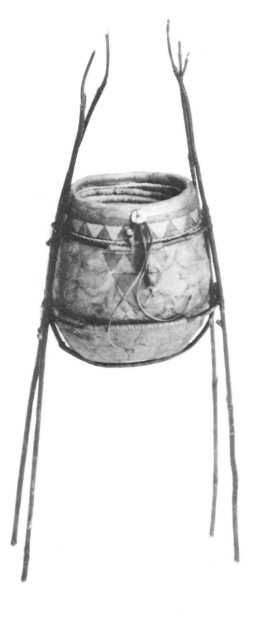

raffia, paper cord, handmade paper, leather, rayon braid, sealing wax, raffia braid, 9"x7", 1984. "Marble Basket," raffia, paper cord, handmade paper, leather, clay marbles, beads, copper wire, raffia braid, 9"x9", 1984. Photos: Rob Karosis. "Pocket Stilt Basket," raffia, paper cord, handmade paper, fabric, watercolor paper, sticks, beads, feathers, thread, 6"x15", 1984. Photo: Color Management Concepts.

Clockwise, from right: "Bone Latch Basket," raffia, paper cord, handmade paper, leather, linen fabric, bone, wood, raffia braid, beads, cane, 9"x7½", 1983. "Saddle Basket,"

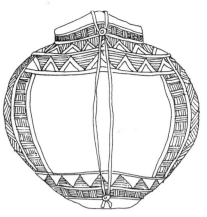

Below: "Sundown Basket,"
raffia, paper cord,
handmade paper, water-
color paper, fabric, leather,
thread, raffia braid,
feathers, beads, 7"x9",
1984. Photo: Craig Blouin.
Sketches by the artist of
work in progress, 1984.

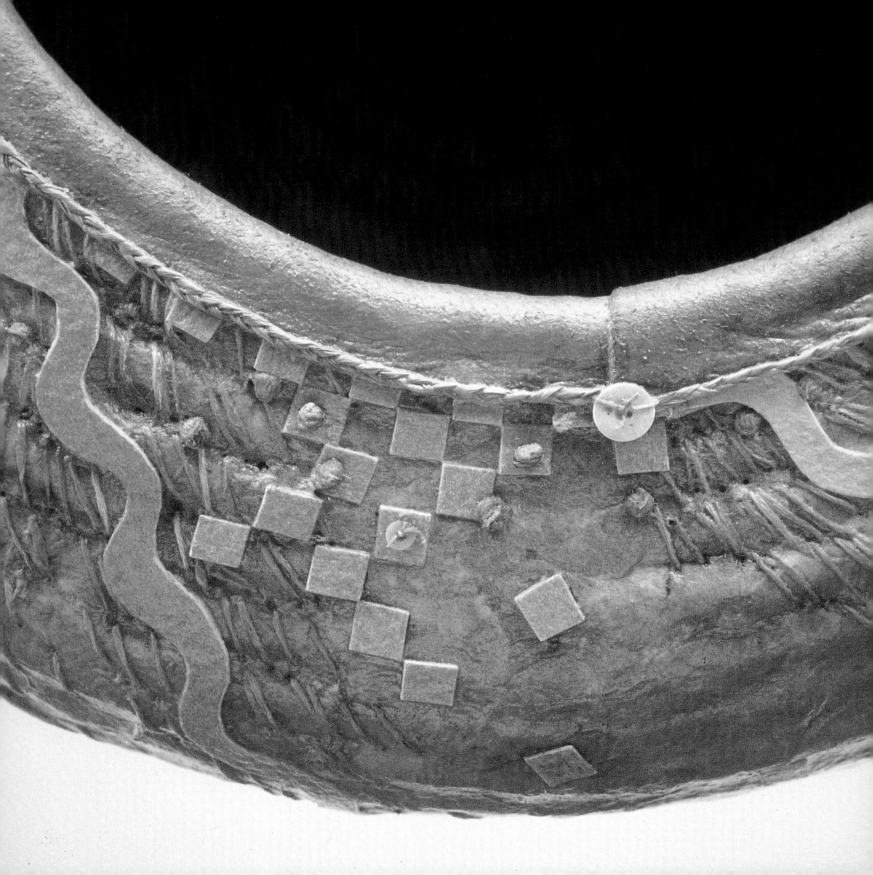

Opposite: Detail of "Halley's Basket," raffia, paper cord, handmade paper, watercolor paper, leather, cotton floss, beads, raffia braid, 9½"x5", 1986.

Below: "As Time Goes By Basket," raffia, paper cord, handmade paper, watercolor paper, beads, thread, 10½"x6¼", 1986. Photos: Stretch Tuemmler.

and objects which have caught my fancy for one reason or another. Occasionally I move them around to see what new combinations I can stir up. For instance, a postcard of a Japanese kimono, photographs of a Navajo blanket and Rousseau's "The Dream" present a provocative combination of histories and sensibilities that can lead to a new image. Sometimes the influence is subliminal and only later do I see the "parts" put together in a drawing. But all of that visual information finds a place somewhere, sometime.

I make both baskets and collages and so I often have quite a few pieces in progress at the same time. This allows the freedom to switch from the tedium of coiling to the more interesting and creative activity of drawing to the satisfying process of finishing a piece all in the same day.

Perhaps my choice of basketmaking as a medium of expression is the synthesis of a background in painting and in textiles. I think of my baskets as two-dimensional surfaces stretched around space. I am "painting" on the surface using the same design elements I would use in a two-dimensional format, the "canvas" just happens to be curved around a basket.

But my choice of basketmaking goes beyond that. I love the materials, the manipulation of those materials. I love the idea of making a functional vessel within an ancient tradition but also extending that tradition. Who's to say that what we do today won't be thought of as traditional in fifty years?

There is something intimate and direct about a basket. The structure is right before you. No tricks, no advanced technology. The forms of my baskets are coiled with raffia over paper cord. Coiling is a traditional technique, its formal possibilities more varied and subtle than some other construction techniques. The surface created, which is solid and closed and relatively even, is then covered with handmade paper and embellished with collaged paper, fabric, leather, stitching, beads, bones, whatever suits the desired image.

Drawing is the mechanism for putting together the mate-

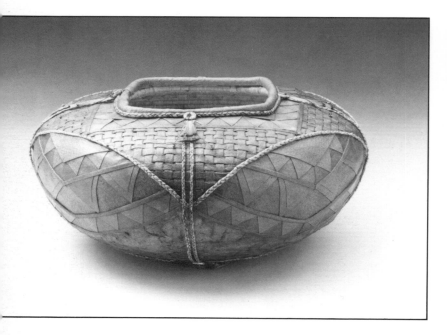

Left: "Circle in the Square Basket," raffia, paper cord, handmade paper, watercolor paper, raffia braid, feathers, thread, beads, 11½"x5½", 1985.
Right: "Six Stitch Basket," paper cord, handmade paper, raffia, raffia braid, beads, thread, 9"x6½", 1985.
Photos: Stretch Tuemmler.

rials, techniques and images that I collect. Many times I don't know where an image is going until the drawing takes me there. It is a curious process that often surprises me and usually pleases me. Occasionally I will see a basket fully finished in my mind's eye and merely record it on paper, but more often the drawing process is integral to the creation of a basket or collage.

Sometimes I work directly on the surface of the basket with no drawing, but this is becoming increasingly rare.

I am not sure where the ideas, the images, come from. Sometimes I feel a little foolish in admitting this. In our age of rational thought, when intelligence is prized over intuition and every question is thought to have an answer, I must say that I truly

am not aware of all the influences which produce the particular combination of color, shape and form of my baskets. An admiration for American Indian and other tribal arts is apparent. But why am I drawn to them in the first place?

My father is a magician. My childhood was punctuated with amazing occurrences which seemed natural to me because

"YooHoo Basket," raffia,
paper cord, handmade
paper, leather, linen fabric,
feathers, cane, beads,
thread, goose wishbone,
11"x14", 1983. Photo:
Rob Karosis.

everything is new and surprising to a child. I didn't realize that my father was any different from anyone's father. As I approached twelve years of age, he was willing to teach me a few of his tricks and I was more than eager to learn them, so I became the sorcerer's apprentice. But before long I realized that being amazed was far more exciting and satisfying than knowing how the trick was done. Magic is magic only when you can't comprehend the illusion.

I feel that way about my work. I don't really want to know where it comes from. The surprise of what comes out is far more exciting and satisfying to me than if I analyzed and researched ethnic or historical sources and could explain their appearance in my baskets. Magic is more fun.

Evening is a lovely time in Maine. The low light contributes to a gentle sunset signalling the end of another day. I try to leave the chaos on my desk in some semblance of order for tomorrow, when I will make another list and coil and draw and make paper and feel fortunate that I can do what I do.

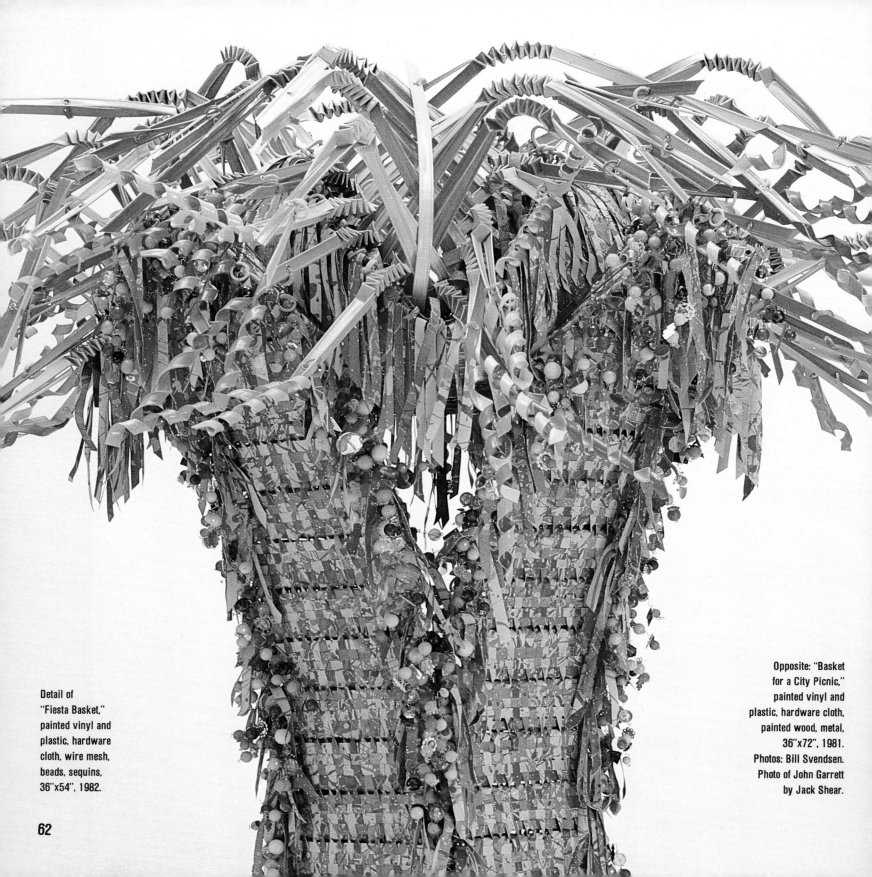

Detail of "Fiesta Basket," painted vinyl and plastic, hardware cloth, wire mesh, beads, sequins, 36"x54", 1982.

Opposite: "Basket for a City Picnic," painted vinyl and plastic, hardware cloth, painted wood, metal, 36"x72", 1981. Photos: Bill Svendsen. Photo of John Garrett by Jack Shear.

62

# JOHN GARRETT

Although I have lived in the Los Angeles metropolitan area for many years, my formative years were spent in the semi-arid desert land of southern New Mexico. The desert environment of my youth influenced my early art work through the natural materials and subtle colors I used. As with textile constructions, the products of elements intermixed to create structure; my basket forms are a mesh of ideas and materials. Living in Los Angeles, I respond not only to the lush, rich plant life superimposed here on a desert biome, but also to the glaring, plastic world of every commercial street. This is one of the reasons I have chosen to work primarily with synthetic materials, products of our technological era. In doing so I take anonymous materials and give them character.

I paint large sheets of fabric-backed vinyl with different colors in a variety of designs. The sheets are then cut into strips. I plait these strips into squares, and also use them to lash spray-painted plastic slats onto wire hardware cloth. The large plaited squares are attached to the lashed construction with plastic-coated wire. I form the basket shape by pulling the four corners of the square toward its

Left: "Zulu Basket," painted vinyl and plastic, hardware cloth, 18"x36", 1981.
Below: "Grandmother's Basket," wire, aluminum, metal screen, plastic clothesline, paint, wire mesh, hardware cloth, 24"x12", 1981. Photos: Bill Svendsen.

center, creating a three-dimensional form with an interior space. I add plastic beads and sequins to the wires. In my current work, I am manipulating rectangular forms into conical forms, and working with prefabricated metal conical armatures as well.

The geometric constructions make reference to screens, fences, lattices and the grid patterns of city streets and high-rise buildings. The designs painted on the vinyl suggest landscapes and atmospheric occurrences. Manipulating the ends of the plastic slats by braiding and with heat, and the addition of beads, sequins, and plastic cord, create curvilinear elements similar to flowers, tendrils and vines. The result is a synthesis of pattern and imagery between that which is geometric and manmade, and the wild, robust organic growth of nature. The synthesized organic materials which were neutralized in processing regain some of their original qualities. Much of my work is festive in quality. Bright colors and reflective surfaces bring to mind parties, fiestas, confetti, city lights, discos, and parades.

"Spider Basket," painted vinyl and plastic, hardware cloth, painted wood, metal, 36"x54", 1981. Photo: Bill Svendsen.

Below: "Wand Basket II," painted vinyl and plastic, hardware cloth, beads, sequins, plastic clothesline, 16"x48", 1985. Photo: Myron Moskwa.
Opposite top: "Time's Heart," bamboo, yarn, palm fiber, hardware cloth, 14"x16", 1983. Photo: Bill Svendsen.
Bottom: "Black Bouquet," painted vinyl and plastic, hardware cloth, beads, sequins, plastic clothesline, 16"x24", 1983. Photo: Bill Svendsen.

The addition of columns or bases constructed of the same materials as support structures for the baskets have further expanded the expressive possibilities of my work. The columns have become tree trunks; yet the square form relates strongly to architectural elements.

Also expanding the possibilities of the baskets is the dialogue between them and the concerns with materials and ideas found in my other work. After making some wire box construction which incorporated plastic toys, I created "Nesting Basket." It is made of everyday, domestic objects: hot pads, clothespins, plastic toys, and a feather duster. This is a basket which is about work, but is certainly not a work basket.

In exploring the expressive character of materials which are not generally used in connection with fiber work, I made a series of wall pieces with steel and aluminum. I used sheets of these metals and cut them into strips. The strips were then lashed to a welded wire grid. I employed these materials and a similar method of construction to creat "Vulcan Purse," a fantasy basket.

I live and work in a one-bedroom duplex on a hill in the Silverlake area of Los Angeles. From the windows of my apartment I can see Sunset Boulevard snaking its way to downtown Los Angeles. I drive several times each week to UCLA, where I teach, through many neighborhoods of varied social strata and ethnic composition. Although I am immersed in this city, I often think of my early life in New Mexico. Indeed, memories of those times often surface in my work. Where lies the relationship between the spines of the cactus and plastic sequins? I love the great foreboding calm of the desert, and I love the electrically charged urban atmosphere where I now live. I see my baskets, and all my work, as an attempt to make whole the disparate experiences and feelings of my life.

# FERNE JACOBS

I have this image: A woman calls me to follow her. I do and we go very far, into another world. This is a world where people are standing still. No one is moving. She tells me to sit down, and I do. She shows me my work. I see pieces of mine and I see some that are unfinished. She tells me to pick up the unfinished work. I do. She then tells me to work, and I do. The people begin to move. It is as if the air begins to circulate again, and life returns to this place.

I would say that this place is a room in my soul. And it is interesting to me that when I work I often have the image that I am making a place for a breath or a stream of air.

Opposite: "Roots," thread and collage, 6"x21½", 1984-85.
Right: "Flame," waxed linen, 5"x48", 1982-83.
Photos: Janice Felgar.
Photo of Ferne Jacobs by Iggy Samuels.

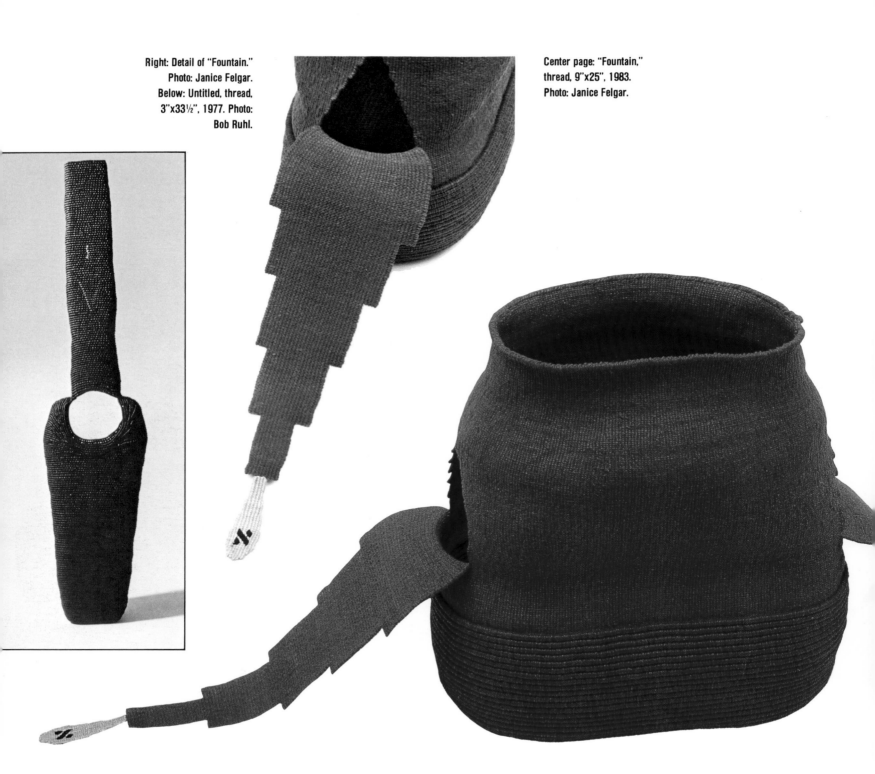

Right: Detail of "Fountain."
Photo: Janice Felgar.
Below: Untitled, thread,
3"x33½", 1977. Photo:
Bob Ruhl.

Center page: "Fountain,"
thread, 9"x25", 1983.
Photo: Janice Felgar.

70

Left: Detail of "Petals."
Below left: "Petals,"
thread, 5¾"x8½", 1984-85.
Below right: "Music,"
thread, 6¾"x9¼", 1984-85.
Photos: Janice Felgar.

# RINA PELEG

"Interweave," ceramic,
4'5"x9', 1985.

I grew up in Israel on a kibbutz. Almost everywhere one walked, one practically stumbled over pottery shards. These fragments are sometimes the only evidence of the rich cultures that existed in the Middle East in the past. My first acquaintance with clay was made through these fragments.

I actually began working with clay after high school, when I discovered the raw material and became aware that almost any shape could be made from the formless mass. At first, I worked with the potter's wheel, making functional pieces to be used at home. I gradually discovered the many possibilities inherent in the material, and began to make explorations in new directions.

Working with clay became a way for me to make contact with the world outside the kibbutz, and, ultimately, outside Israel.

While attending university, I worked on hand-coiled clay structures that involved a play of unconnected coils within the structures. This experience taught me that a coil could be used the way rope or string is used in weaving and plaiting, and I began to "weave" with these

clay coils. Since the woven coils were basically the same kind of coils I had used for traditional pinched pots, the transition was simple and involved only a slight change in technique. My weaving experience made this a natural transition for me.

The clay baskets I am doing

now are made up of plaited coils which are not pinched. The final shape is strong, yet light in feeling. The clay basket "breathes" as a natural basket would.

The connection between basketry and working in clay is, all in all, a very natural one. Both clay and the straw used in

73

Left: Rina Peleg working on "Farrago."
Below: "Farrago," low-fire stoneware, 4'x5', 1985.
Opposite: "Yellow Gold Art II," clay, 18"x31", 1981.

making baskets are materials man has used for ages.

The commonly held theory is that the first clay container came about when a hole was dug in the (clay) ground and a fire made in it. After the fire was put out, it was discovered that the sides of the hole had been, in fact, fired. The hole had become a container for anything, including water. The next step, obviously, was to "remove" the hole from the earth by cutting around it, leaving enough clay to make the new shape self-supporting and portable.

Eventually, it was discovered that the best way to make a pot was not to remove a hole, but to create the structure from clay coils pinched together. The idea of using coils presumably came from baskets. An imprint of a basket made of coils was found in the clay floor of a home in Jericho from 7000 BC, a time when ceramics was in its infancy (there are no pots dating from that period).

The idea of making clay baskets is also connected to the ancient custom of imprinting mats or other woven material into the surface of clay pots

Double wall basket, clay,
28"x18", 1980.

tional objects with which we are all familiar. However, the works were made without any function in mind.

I have been concerned for several years with the so-called right of the ceramist to create non-functional works. My own reason for making such works was, and is, a strong attraction to the basic, classical shapes. This clearly came about from a deep emotional need, not practical intent.

I began to understand some of the sources from which I drew my ideas upon learning about Jung's theory of the collective unconscious. Jung maintains that there is a collective unconscious of the whole human race which manifests itself in each individual through that person's dreams, or, as in my case, through creativity. The basic shapes of ceramic utensils which were used ages ago, as well as the technique of making them, form part of the collective unconscious.

My need to make the shapes I do can be explained in part, if such explanation is necessary, by Jung's theory, my own acquaintance with the history of arts and crafts, and a strong personal need.

before they were fired. Baskets were also used as molds which were later burned with the clay. Coils resembling rope are often found as decorative elements on early pots. Large pots in ancient Egypt often had no handles and were carried in large baskets, much the way some Mexicans and Africans carry their wares to

the market today.

A final example of the affinity between clay and basketry is the fact that clay and straw were probably the first materials used to make huts. The inside of these primitive structures was covered with slip and later burnished. The outside was covered with woven straw mixed with clay

which stopped the rain from coming in.

Weaving in clay has become a natural activity for me. The difference between my pieces and the traditional, functional works made of clay or straw is that the pieces I make are quite impractical. At first glance, my work seems to relate to func-

76

Left: Woven clay structure,
porcelain, 25"x38", 1983.
Right: "Yellow Gold Art I," clay,
18"x31", 1981.

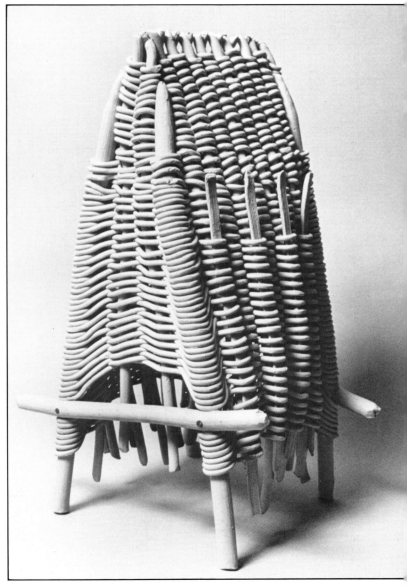

# KARYL SISSON

My work is an exploration of the physical and metaphorical possibilities that result when materials, structure and form interact. Over the years, I have rummaged through basements, garage sales and junk stores, salvaging cloth, sewing notions and related elements from domestic life. These have provided the inspiration for my sculptures. Presently, my focus is the transformation of familiar objects through the building of form.

The zippers, clothespins and twill tape serve as building materials, while any number of basketry and needlework techniques provide the methods of construction. The basic structures are developed by interlocking the materials; no glue, nails or internal supports are used. Because the structures are flexible, they can be manipulated in various ways to create different forms which are linked to my interest in ancient and indigenous architecture, organic growth, and patterns in nature.

After traveling to the Yuca-

Photos of Karyl Sisson and her work by Myron Moskwa.

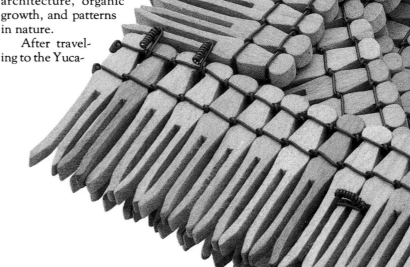

78

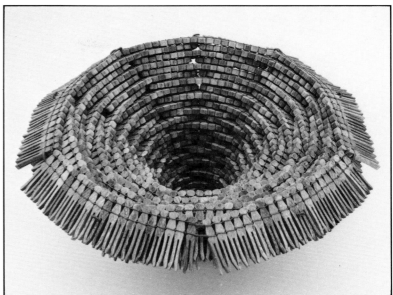

Right: "Container III," stained wooden clothespins, wire, 18"x9", 1984.
Below: "Container V," stained wooden clothespins, wire, 15"x6", 1985.

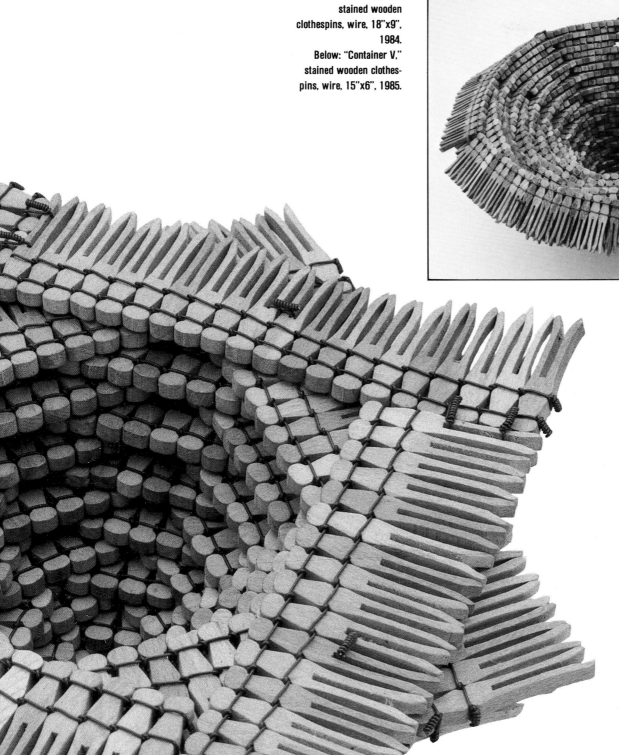

tan and experiencing Chichen Itza, I began making small pyramids constructed solely of clothespins and wire. By inverting the pyramid, I discovered a container form which exposed more of the pin and revealed an interior surface and space quite different from the exterior surface and shape. I was intrigued, and began working with my particular palette of materials to create other container forms. These have become another vehicle for me to explore personal and formal issues. What I find important is the aesthetic and suggestive quality of the form, rather than whether the form is defined as or serves as a functional object.

Clothespins and zippers are simple inventions that have endured in our complex society. My sculptures seek to mirror the beauty and simplicity of these individual elements.

79

Right: Side view of
"Container III."
Top: "Container II,"
wooden clothespins, wire,
19"x8", 1984.
Bottom: "Vessel IV," dyed
zippers, stained wooden
clothespins, 18"x10",
1985.

Left: "Vessel II," zippers, stained wooden clothespins, 18"x14", 1985.
Below: "Vessel III," dyed zippers, stained wooden clothespins, 16"x12", 1985.

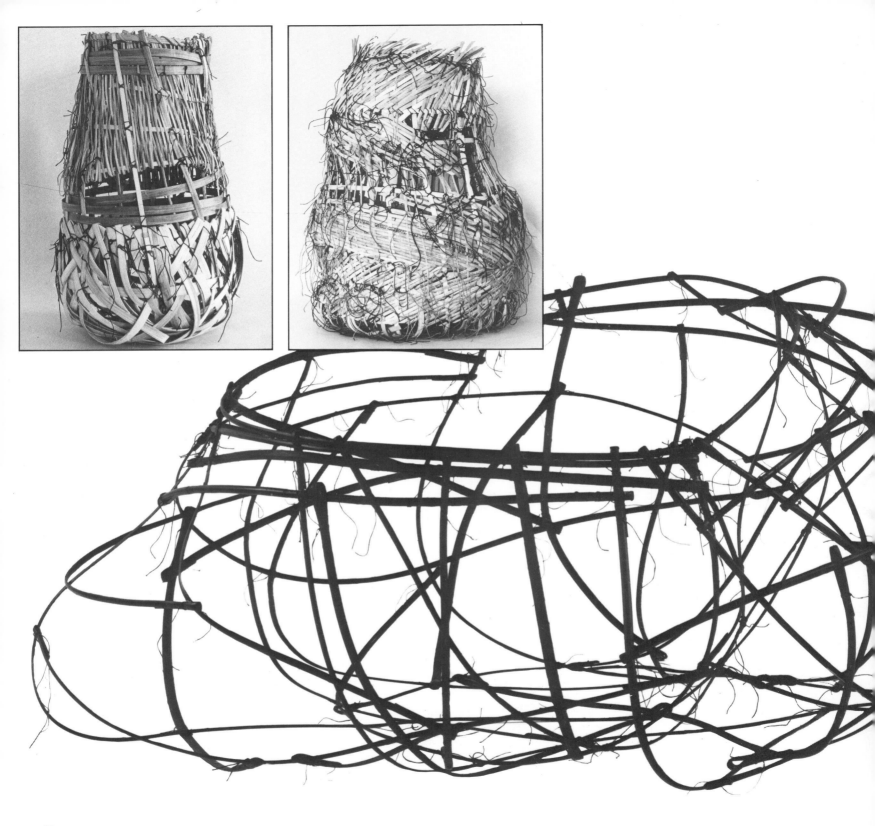

# LILLIAN ELLIOTT

I'm not exactly sure when I began making baskets. I had been weaving flat tapestries for years. It was as though my sense of volume had been developing in secret while I worked on the flat surface. I was amazed to discover that I loved working in the round. I was elated at being able to work on large forms. Making baskets was like taking the best of ceramics, drawing, and textiles; it was direct, expansive, and it could even be meditative. One of the nice features was that I could work over the whole surface of an object simultaneously, and not from top to bottom as I do in weaving. Unlike tapestries, baskets didn't take years to finish.

Opposite top left: "Hayfield," rattan, linen, acrylic, 10"x19", 1981.
Opposite top right: "Tag Ends," reed, bamboo, linen, 15"x25", 1979.
Center: "Drawn Form," rattan, acrylics, linen, 48"x26", 1984.
Photo: Scott McCue.
Photo of Lillian Elliott by Roy Elliott.

Opposite left: "Yi Dynasty," rattan,
linen, acrylics, 17"x25", 1985.
Opposite right: "Shrine," reed,
linen, paper, coconut mid-rib,
42"x42", 1981.
Below: "Feather Basket," plastic
tape, wire, 15"x12", 1979.

I began by buying strong cord that had a lot of spring. Without untying the package of cord I tied a number of strands together. Then, I cut here and there, and tied down again. I continued this procedure until I could see a form emerging from this mass, or mess, in front of me. Next, I bought a package of glossy, brilliantly dyed raffia. I twined the outer layer together, and began to hollow out the inside, as I might have done with clay, until what was left was a small, rather precious raffia bundle with a hollow core, a kind of simple basket. By this time I was hooked.

Then I did a series of large baskets, binding and tying, regarding the lines I made as drawings, simultaneously describing the inner structure and the outer shape. In the beginning I wanted the material to speak for itself. I was reluctant to direct it too much. Later, I came to enjoy making a strong statement, and the question of imposing my will just didn't seem to be an issue any longer.

I decided to work on a three-dimensional piece that would try to make a strong statement. I

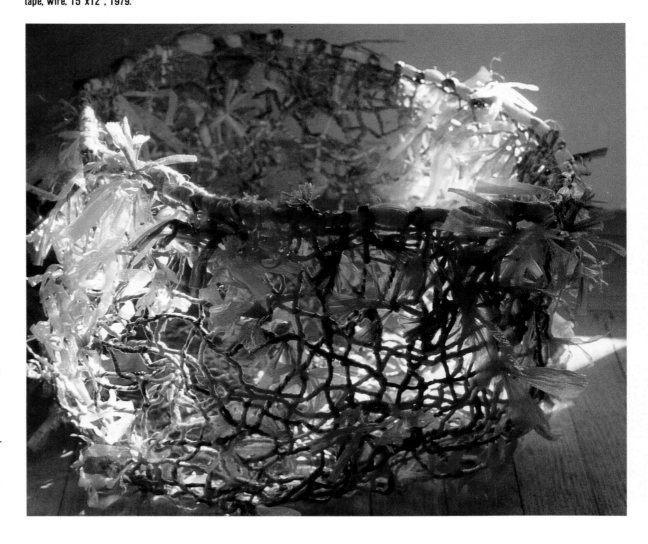

Above: "Romany," mixed
materials, 5'x8'2"x6'7",
1985. Collaboration with
Pat Hickman. Photo:
Scott McCue.
Opposite left: "Boxed
Basket," branches,
acrylics, linen,
8"x24", 1982.
Opposite right: "Blackline
Basket," rattan, linen,
acrylics, 18"x20", 1981.

mixed a number of materials together, and painted the piece black when I finished. It was so strong that at one point in the construction it actually frightened me. I called it "Goya," because it has some of the intensity of the "Horrors of War" series. This is one of the few baskets of that time that continues to interest me.

I think of my baskets as describing volume, as if I were drawing on the surface of very specific concrete forms. I think

of the form inside as pushing out the outside walls. The elements and shapes of my baskets are like skeletal structures, and often I paint them black to reinforce that impression. I see them as calligraphic shapes or gestural drawings. They aren't drawings, they are baskets, but they move in space describing where one perceived shape ends and another begins.

As for technique, I mostly use twining because it holds together dissimilar elements,

because it makes such a strong structure, and because I twine without being conscious of the technique. Sometimes, I also use knotting or binding. I don't much care what techniques are used. I'm concerned with the form and impact, that is, the visual impact of the work. I feel the same way regardless of the medium I work in.

My work has included collaborating on baskets with Pat Hickman. I construct the form, and Pat covers the surface. At every stage we consult about the results. Those baskets have a very different character from the ones I do alone. The most obvious difference is that there is always a surface on the collaborative work. The baskets I do alone are generally linear, often black, and usually rather complicated.

I'm interested in combining manmade and natural materials, although I've not done much of it so far. I think that I've been more adventurous with form than I have been up till now with materials. I'm interested in using more color. I once saw a traveling exhibit of Korean folk art and could hardly wait to paint

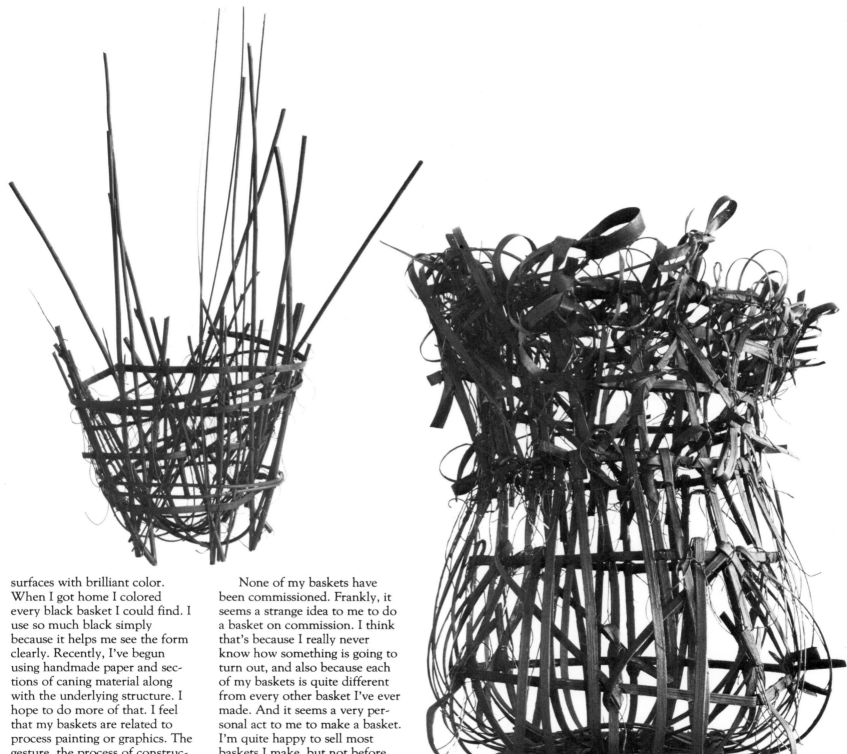

surfaces with brilliant color. When I got home I colored every black basket I could find. I use so much black simply because it helps me see the form clearly. Recently, I've begun using handmade paper and sections of caning material along with the underlying structure. I hope to do more of that. I feel that my baskets are related to process painting or graphics. The gesture, the process of construction is an important aspect of the final work.

None of my baskets have been commissioned. Frankly, it seems a strange idea to me to do a basket on commission. I think that's because I really never know how something is going to turn out, and also because each of my baskets is quite different from every other basket I've ever made. And it seems a very personal act to me to make a basket. I'm quite happy to sell most baskets I make, but not before I've made them. I think it would cramp my style.

# MARY MERKEL-HESS

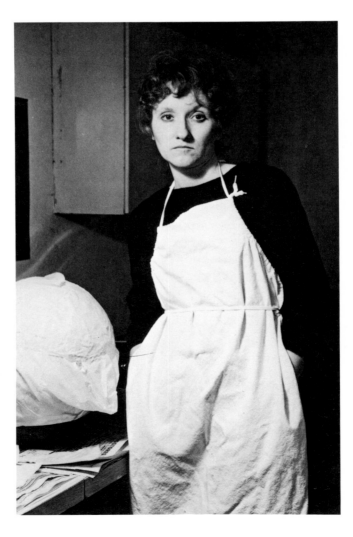

Until a few years ago I worked only as a metalsmith. I began making baskets in response to some things I was doing in metal. It was a case of a sudden inspiration causing me to leap into another medium. At the time, I was completing my graduate work in metal, and was folding metal and trying to recreate natural forms in a spontaneous way. I realized that I was imagining things that could be done more effectively with paper. It was an idea I couldn't resist, and in a few restless weeks of experimenting I developed the technique that I used to make my first baskets. It was a papier-mache technique utilizing a variety of glues and many layers of very thin paper applied over a mold. There were paper cord inclusions that strengthened the baskets and created a pattern on the interior surface. The first baskets were ribbed, and had ruffled leaf-like edges. They were both a contrast to and a further exploration of the ideas I had been working on in metal. The freedom the paper gave me was heady and the response to the paper vessels was positive. I had

many ideas to explore. I continued making the baskets, and what had begun as a short-term project became a major involvement.

These first baskets were inspired by natural phenomena, the grasses, flowers, and life along the roadsides in my native Iowa. I grew up in rural, weedy places and then left to live in a city for ten years. When I returned to the country I was overwhelmed by the grassy memories of my childhood. I was interested in sticks and deeply folded plant leaves, and the paper was perfect for recreating these forms. The colors I used were natural and the paper cord inclusions looked like natural fiber. As I became more interested in basketry itself, there were references to traditional baskets, mainly woven patterns embedded in the paper. I have great appreciation for basketry, but little knowledge of traditional techniques.

During the next year I made many baskets at the same time that I continued to work in metal, always making vessels. Container forms have interested me from the very beginning of

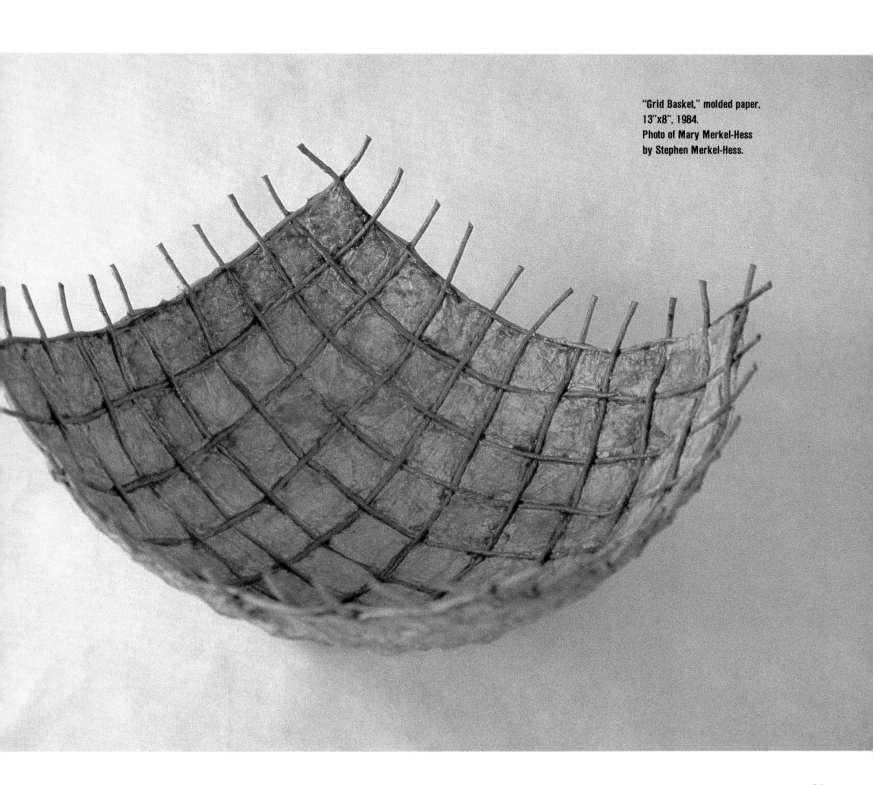

"Grid Basket," molded paper,
13"x8", 1984.
Photo of Mary Merkel-Hess
by Stephen Merkel-Hess.

my art career. It was that interest that led me to crafts, to metalsmithing and eventually to baskets. I like the fact that all sorts of containers, made of all sorts of materials, are part of our daily lives. They are so elemental. I always imagine that some kind of vessel was the very first tool of our species. In some prehistoric dawn an ancestor picked up a shell to carry water or used a hollow gourd to gather food. For me, vessels seem inextricably linked to what it means to be human. I think simpler societies felt this more keenly than we do. At least their ritual utensils for religious ceremonies have more importance than similar objects do in our society. But then, we think of many kinds of containers as art objects, which is also a way of conferring importance.

At the same time that I was making baskets with references to plant life, I was doing drawings of flowers, seed pods, and grasses as a means to visual understanding and inspiration. I kept a notebook and covered quite a bit of other paper with drawing and watercolor painting. It occurred to me that I was

Above: "Shadows of Flowers (3)," paper, wood, 6"x7", 1985.
Opposite top left: "Intoxicated with Shadows of Flowers," paper, wood, 10"x18", 1985.
Opposite top right: "Waving Grasses Basket," molded paper, 7"x14", 1983.
Opposite bottom: "Lotus," molded paper, 20"x8", 1983.

making drawings on paper and then making baskets of paper. Perhaps there could be a more direct connection. I began to use my drawings in the actual basketmaking. I rolled up some of my drawings. I was delighted with the delicate rolls, and the clues along their edges of the drawings inside. At first, I inserted the drawings through the center of the molded baskets. This led not only to more drawing but also more insertions—sticks, painted dowels, and wrapped wands. When I inserted something through the center of the basket I was challenging its function directly. Previously, the interior of a vessel had seemed inviolable to me—the space inside was the essence of its container-ness. But so often, when my baskets were displayed, they were hung with the interior surface outward. Even baskets that were quite deep were hung in this way and I began to feel that this space was mine to use. The interior of the basket became like a canvas to me—an area set apart for artistic composition. I experimented by piercing the baskets with rolls of paper or sticks, always trying to

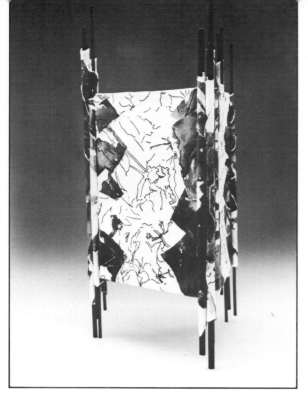

play the straightness and pattern of those elements off the curvilinear surface of the basket.

While I was first piercing baskets, I was also making another, quite different attempt to use my drawings directly in container-making. For these pieces I constructed a box of paper board and then covered it with fragments of a drawing. I chose a box shape because I wanted something archetypal, but not in any way earthy. The boxes have simple, geometric shapes that are entirely covered with drawing—on the interior as well as the exterior. The drawing-covered box is a repository for my visual feelings about a subject, an icon. When I have more drawings than I need to cover a box, I roll them up and attach them to the sides. I think of these paper vessels not only as icons, but also as three-dimensional drawings, much abstracted in their final form. The way they look may make them seem like a departure from my other baskets, but they are not. The boxes are another way of dealing with the same visual phenomena that inspired my first baskets.

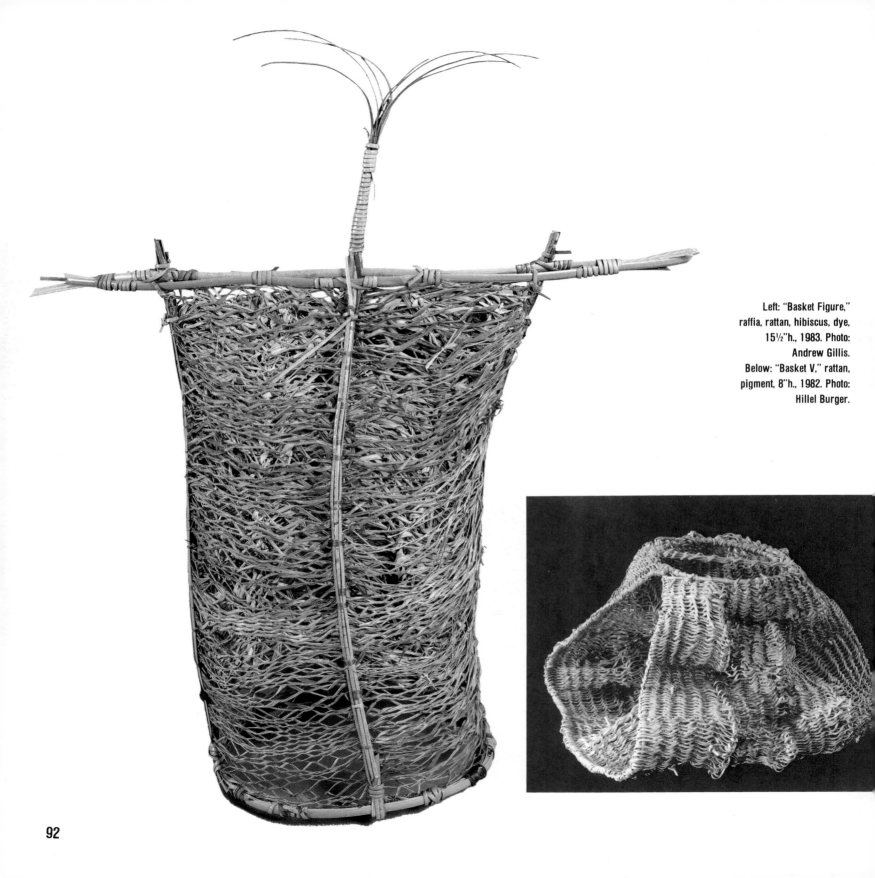

Left: "Basket Figure,"
raffia, rattan, hibiscus, dye,
15½"h., 1983. Photo:
Andrew Gillis.
Below: "Basket V," rattan,
pigment, 8"h., 1982. Photo:
Hillel Burger.

# JOANNE SEGAL BRANDFORD

I am not a basketmaker. My "baskets" are not really baskets. I think they are *images* of baskets.

For many years I have used netting technique to investigate light and space. With the "baskets" my goal was to bring an increased sense of volume to the nets, and to have them stand up on their own, independent, defying gravity.

I enjoy the directness of knotless and knotted netting. To make a net I simply begin, with minimal equipment and with no theoretical encumbrance. I bring idea to material as easily as pencil to paper.

The intimate nature of the process is also important to me. A net builds relatively slowly, one loop at a time, as I bring the active end of a working strand through a previously constructed loop. This encourages very close, moment-by-moment involvement. The creation of each new mesh demands active participation, with mental awareness and physical control. While working in the present, I must, at the same time, review and test what has gone before. I appreciate this direct and complex flow between

mind, eye, hand, material, front and back, past and present.

Making nets is like writing or musical composition. Words and notes, like the loops of a net, may appear to interconnect in simple and linear fashion, yet complexity and beauty are always possible.

These net "baskets" are the products of a three-way (material/method/me) conversation. Occasionally I have gone too far, stubbornly refusing to acknowledge material/method limits. At these times I have retreated, to repair, support, and revise. The trick is to know when to stop.

Photo of Joanne Segal Brandford by Andrew Gillis.

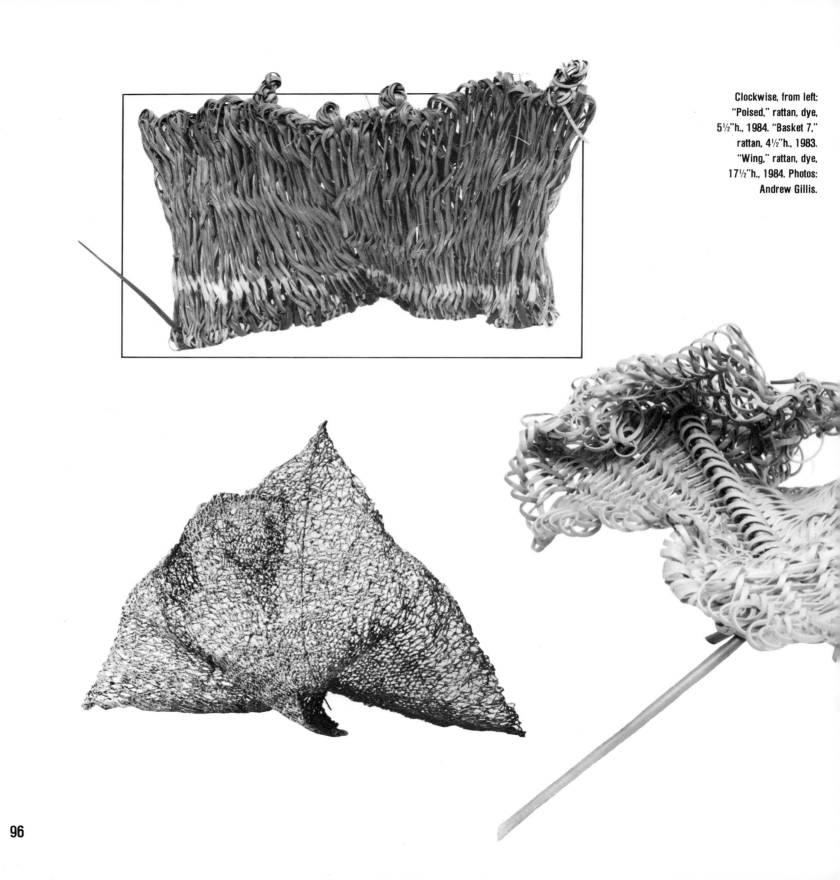

"Brown Net," raffia, hibiscus, rattan, dyes, 7"h., 1983. Photo: Andrew Gillis.

# MICHAEL DAVIS

I n college I studied ceramics and painting, then I worked as a graphic artist and illustrator. I was dissatisfied with the creative progress in my painting and pottery, and knew that my emergence as an artist depended upon finding an avenue of expression that better suited my abilities.

My life as a fiber artist began quite by chance. I had taken a new job with a company whose offices were on the second floor of a gracefully restored Victorian house. On the first floor was a retail fiber shop, through which I had to pass to get to my office. The shop was a feast for the senses, filled with looms, hand-spun yarns, fleece, spinning wheels of all shapes and sizes, reeds, grasses, and materials from the world over, in a myriad of colors. This was my initial exposure to the fiber arts, and made me realize I had found my niche as an artist.

My formal instruction in basketry was through that shop, a class in the Appalachian style of weaving. I spent two years perfecting Appalachian forms before experimenting with color. I was amazed that with subtle structural changes these utilitarian baskets could become sculpture-like forms. I also realized that one could spend a lifetime on a single Appalachian form, creating endless interpretations.

To further develop my craft, and because of limitations of Appalachian forms, I began working with wicker, using the twining technique. I achieved fluidity by using very small ribs and weavers, and created sculp-ted architectural forms through control of the tension between the ribs and weavers.

Generally, I work on several baskets simultaneously, and spend eight to ten hours a day in my studio. This way of working keeps my interest at a maximum, provides stimulation, and strengthens the work in progress.

Sometimes I make preliminary sketches, especially for commissioned pieces, when sketches are used for the initial

Left: "Mahogany," dyed reed,
Plexiglas, 11"x13", 1985. Photo:
Jettie Griffin.
Below: "Namibia," dyed reed,
acrylic paint, 19"x32", 1985.
Photo: Daryl Bunn.
Photo of Michael Davis by
Jettie Griffin.

Left: "Texture 11," unspun
canton rope, 12"x12",
1984.
Right: "Wooly Bully," dyed
reed, unspun hemp,
Plexiglas, 14"x15", 1985.
Photos: Daryl Bunn.

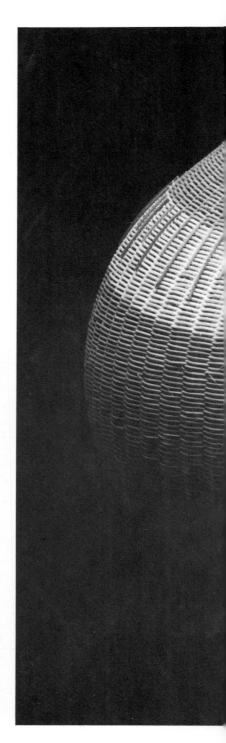

presentations. At other times I
begin with a mental picture of
what I want to achieve, and then
let the controlled and uncon-
trolled weaving processes take
over. Some of my most striking
baskets have resulted from this

approach. Availability of a material sometimes forces me to
rethink a design. I may substitute
new color or texture—or both—
in order to maintain the integrity
of the piece.

In my recent works I have

been using geometric and
abstract patterning imposed
upon sculptural shapes, empha-
sizing color and achieving a
multi-dimensional quality. I
manipulate color through dye
mixing, applied acrylic and

"Form Series 11," dyed
reed, Plexiglas, glue,
14"x17", 1985. Photo:
Daryl Bunn.

enamel paints, and a pointillism technique I've adapted for basketry. My shapes are deliberate and architectural.

My background in pottery has had a strong impact on my work, as has my interest in the work of tribal artisans. At one time I worked in a museum, and developed a profound interest in primitive tribal art. I was fascinated with the ceremonial masks and symbolic fiberworks. I spent every spare moment studying the exhibits of African and Indian work, especially the basketry.

I use intricate methods to add textural interest to a piece. The process is painstaking and time-consuming. For example, on one of my recent baskets I've applied over 2000 pieces of painted, clipped pine needles.

Sophistication of design, skill of technique, and refinement of execution are my aims in the exploration of basketry as an art form. In my work, frustration and exhilaration merge as I find myself reconciling opposing forces. This duality—this dichotomy—is resolved through the harmonious interplay of opposites: the old versus the new, restraint versus freedom, the natural versus the manmade, simplicity versus complexity. These conflicts and their resolution form the basis of my work.

There is a responsibility that comes with increased exposure and recognition. I continually study the field of fiber. I maintain a file on fiber artists who have shown in the last six to eight years. I keep an up-to-date notebook with names of galleries that advertise nationally, particularly those that have shown fiber recently, to provide me with leads as to possible markets.

I believe that, as basketmakers, we have a commitment to galleries, collectors, museums, and the public, to produce more complex and original works. I also feel that basketry should be promoted to a greater degree, as are other art forms. The idea of fiber as a fine art form is now being increasingly accepted by the contemporary arts community. There's an air of change and a growing awareness of the aesthetic possibilities of fiber arts. However, fiber commands insufficient interest and understanding from the art establishment, and consequently, from the public.

Left: "Pluto," dyed reed, enamel paint, Plexiglas, 17"x23", 1986.
Right: "Spiritual Ritualism," dyed reed, Plexiglas, acrylic paint, 17"x24", 1986. Photos: Daryl Bunn.

"Indian Summer," dyed
reed, pine needles,
Plexiglas, 16"x24", 1985.
Photo: Daryl Bunn.

# MARIAN HAIGH-NEAL

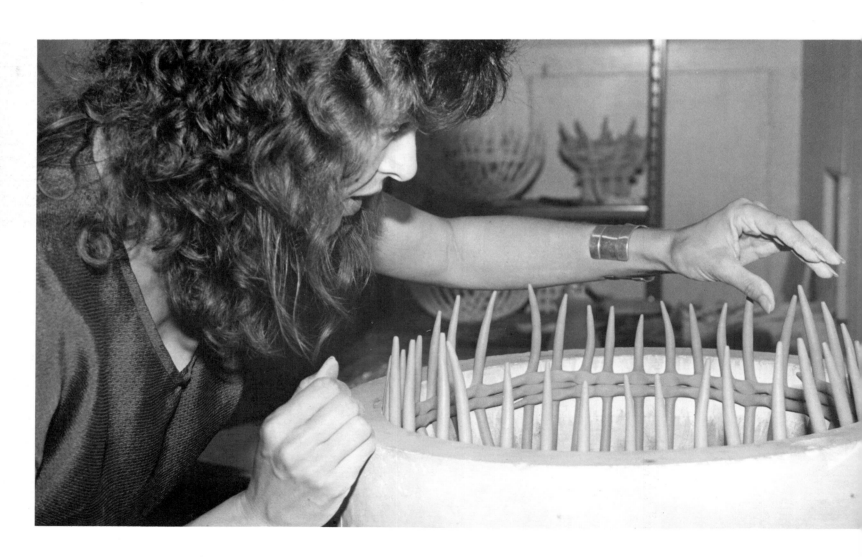

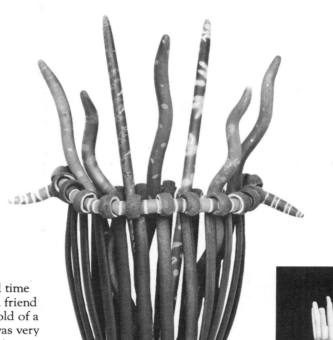

B y 1979, I had been working in clay full time for several years. A friend gave me a large plaster mold of a hemisphere shape and I was very intrigued. I had been looking at some Italian majolica basketlike flower pots. So I decided to make some coils and experiment with the new round form. I loved the pure, sparse shape that resulted, and I was hooked on basketry.

The idea for a new basket starts slowly in my mind as a shape, color, or feeling. Occasionally I may have enough of an idea to actually sketch something on paper. More often I simply work with some shapes of clay, or coils, or sticks, and place them in ways I've never seen in order to strengthen that feeling I'm looking for. I have never used baskets as a direct influence, only as a departure for my forms. My influences are bones, landscapes, bare trees, coral, vines, thorns, ceremonial objects and rituals.

I have always been fascinated by ancient civilizations and their costumes, ceremonial objects, and everyday implements. There has, for me, always been a sense of what rich cultures lay in the past.

This richness I also find through nature in the twisting honeysuckle vines and cut-aways in hills that reveal different strata of rock, clay and colored earth. The landscape of the Southwest, where I have lived and explored for many years, is a very strong influence in my work. I love the vast open spaces, rolling hills, windswept trees, rivers, canyons, mountains and occasional bleached bones lying on the ground. This sometimes sparse landscape full of hidden strength is something I try to bring to my work.

My "Seagrass Basket" developed over a period of two years. One spring I spent a week on a tiny island on a coral reef and snorkled in the ocean for the first time. Even now I find it difficult to say how I was affected by the color and movement of the coral and fish suddenly before my eyes. The sound of the water lapping at my ears and my magnified breathing heightened the sense of a totally new world. When I came home all I had was a memory of those things. Eventually, I developed a pastel glaze I thought was suitable and added it to a basket form with wavy tines. This basket helps me recall my beautiful experience under water in another world.

I have always worked somewhat sporadically in my clay studio, partly because I have had to hold down part-time jobs from time to time and also because it seems to be a normal work cycle for me. Sometimes I spend several weeks or months thinking I'm not making any progress in my work. I have come to learn that most of the time I am processing information inside. This inner processing feels uncomfortable if it lasts a very long time. I continue other work I can do without much emotional investment.

Finally the new idea starts coming together, and I may be on a creative run for several months with ideas spinning out in many directions. Then after a period of time I scrap the new pieces which have not worked

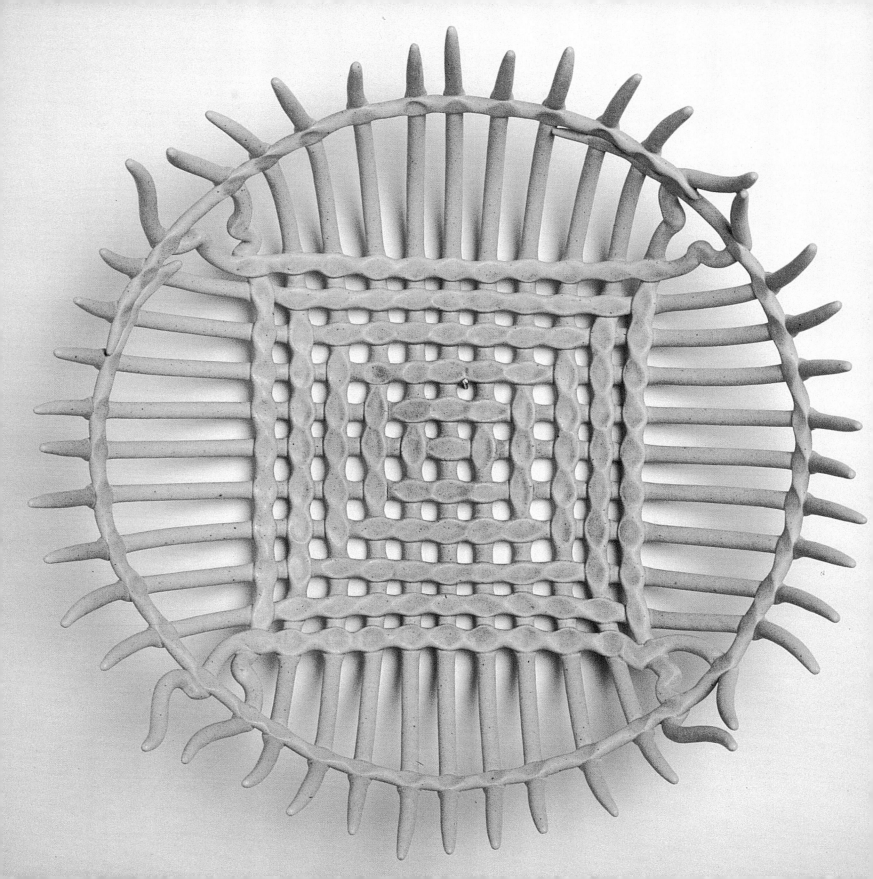

technically or have not fulfilled
the idea I had in mind. Most of
my rejects end up in the shard
pile at the base of the "wailing
wall" outside my studio door.
Occasionally I keep a piece that
didn't work, because it may lead
me to a new series. It might have
just a germ of an idea I need to
look at for a while, perhaps for
several years.

In 1984 I began looking for a
shape different from the round
form. I had always been interested in curvy, snakelike forms,
and in a fit of boredom made a
number of curved fat coils with
smoothly tapered ends. Then I
sat in my studio looking at all
my new snakelike coils, wondering why I had made them and,
more to the point, what I was
going to *do* with them. So I just
played around, and I painted
stripes and designs on some of
the coils and refined them. Then
I had a friend throw some large
bowl forms on his wheel for me
to use as new molds. I experimented and learned that with a
few tricks I could suspend basketlike forms from previously fired
clay structures. This has allowed
me to build larger, stronger
pieces in steps.

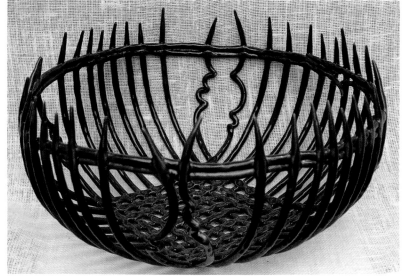

My black and gray colored
baskets are fired in an electric
kiln in a saggar with sawdust.
During the firing, the sawdust
heats to burning, but only
smolders and smokes because
the saggar chamber has a lid that
has cut off most of the oxygen. It
is the smoking sawdust, or
reduction atmosphere, which
gives the clay its characteristic
color range. The baskets that I
build in stages and finish in sawdust are fired from three to
seven times each.

Baskets throughout history
and even present day have acted
as helpers to mankind. It is usual
for a basket to be constructed

Left: "Wall Grid," glazed
stoneware and slip decorations,
15"x15", 1981. Photo:
Randy Ehrlich.
Below: "Fish Trap Basket," glazed
stoneware, 17"x19", 1984. Photo:
Rick Patrick.
Right: "Black Speckled Basket,"
glazed stoneware, 13"x9", 1985.
Photo: Rick Patrick.

with the themes of beauty and
function in mind. I am interested
in beauty and other ideas as well.
It is common for snake imagery,
sharp tines, and thorns to surface in my work. It is fun for me
to make a lovely, pastel colored
"thorn basket" that contains an
element of danger suggested by
the sharp thorns. I am reminded
of picking succulent blackberries
to eat but having to watch carefully for thorns and snakes. It is
not to say I find snakes and
thorns bad things; quite the con-
trary: I celebrate them. These
additional nuances in my work
are the reminders of the capri-
ciousness of life we see about us
every day.

"Thorn Basket," with its reference to vines and thorns, and
"Bone Basket" are my most
recently completed baskets. I am
still excited about building a
form in pieces and watching it
change through all the firings.

My newest work once again
seems to be processing within. In
the meantime I am working on
some small landscape-like sculptures that hold small basins in
their surfaces. I am looking at
wood formations and listening to
my dreams at night.

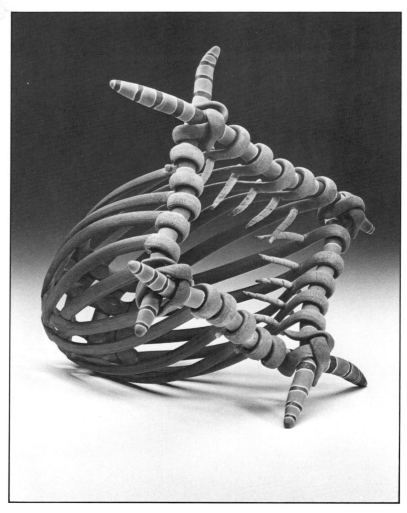

# DOUGLAS E. FUCHS

**M**y work reflects a long preoccupation with structure, form and control of materials. Beginning in 1978 I was taken with a cylindrical shape, quite totemic and phallic in nature. Originally wall hung, these forms began to dictate a life of their own. Legs developed, and my "spirit totems" were born. These smaller attempts led to "Forest Group" in 1980, and ultimately to "Sky Towers," an eighteen-foot form woven at Artpark in August, 1980. This imagery coalesced in "Floating Forest," a monumental fiber environment that contained seven woven totem forms ranging in height from six to thirteen feet, and a variety of other fiber constructions, all made of indigenous

Left: "Floating Forest Totem Group" and "Survivor," reeds, raffia, sea grass, pods, palm stalks, aloe stalks, 8-9'h., 1981. Photo of Doug Fuchs by Catherine Snedecker.

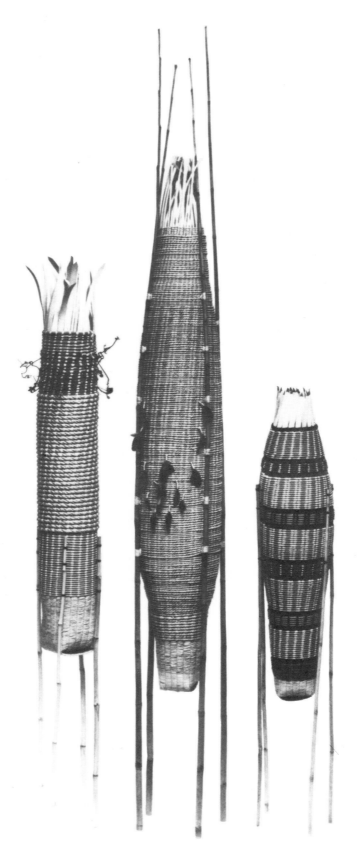

Australian materials. This work was commissioned by the Australian Crafts Council on a fellowship that involved living with the Aborigines, researching their baskets and teaching contemporary basketry all over Australia. An exciting and demanding year!

On my way home I traveled in Indonesia and Southeast Asia, notably Bali and Thailand. I was thunderstruck with color and festive vitality wherever I went. After returning home I began to work with dyed, painted, and synthetic materials, in a new series: "Chedis," forms inspired by Thai temples. This work evolved to "Quiet Cone" an eighteen-foot installation for a show at the Bronx Museum (and currently in the collection of the Museum of Contemporary Craft). I continued to make cone forms until a serious illness disabled me.

I see the body of my work as an expanding search for a spiritual sensibility in the fiber to which I am very drawn. I feel that it works as a body of symbolic form and emotion. It helped lead me into the world of international sensibility and a greater openness to life.

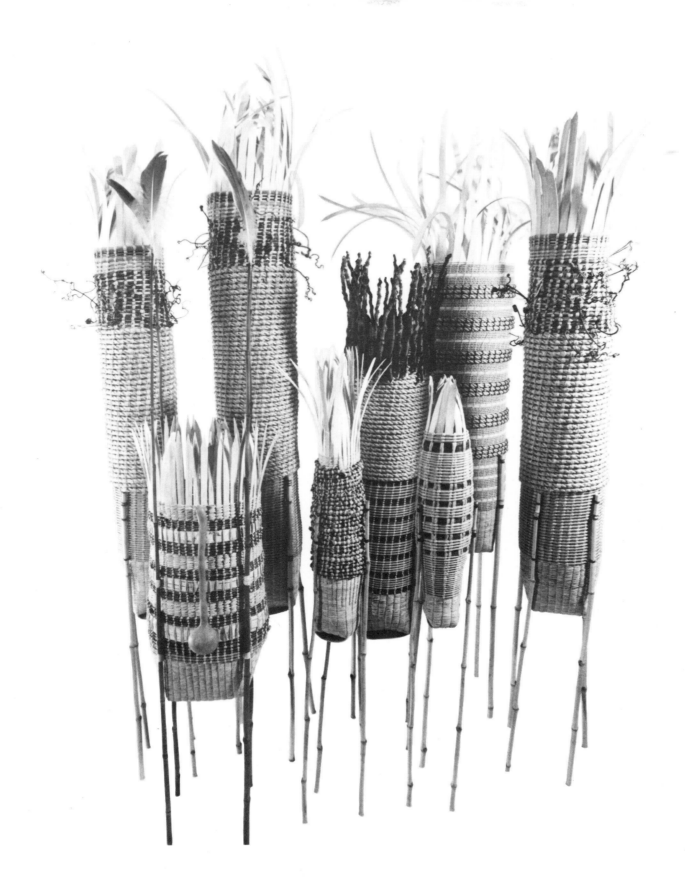

Opposite left: "Spirit
Baskets," raffia, reed, bone,
beads, feathers, 5'h., 1979.
Opposite right, from left:
"Tall Totem with
Tendrils," 4½'h. "Parrot
Totem," 7'h. "Painted
Totem 1," 4'h., reed, raffia,
sea grass, bamboo,
feathers, 1980-81.
Left: "Forest Totems," flat
reed, rolled paper, raffia,
grapevine, manila rope,
birch bark, twigs, bamboo,
3-6'h., 1981.

Above: "Sky Poles," plastic
stripping, PVC-coated rayon,
copper wire, 8'h., 1984.
Right: "Rainbow Forest," plastic
stripping, PVC-coated rayon,
copper wire, pin heads,
14"h., 1984.
Opposite: "Chedis/Cones," reed,
sea grass, plastic-coated wire,
dyes, paints, 3-4'h., 1983.

"Spirit Guide" from "Floating Forest."

Opposite: "Floating Forest," reed, raffia, sea grass, sisal rope, leather stripping, tarred jute, pods, palm stalks, aloe stalks, pine wood, bamboo, paper bark, 1981.
Near right: "Sleeping Creature in Dream Vessel" from "Floating Forest," paper bark, palm fiber, palm branches, tarred jute, pine, willow.
Far right: Detail from "Floating Forest."

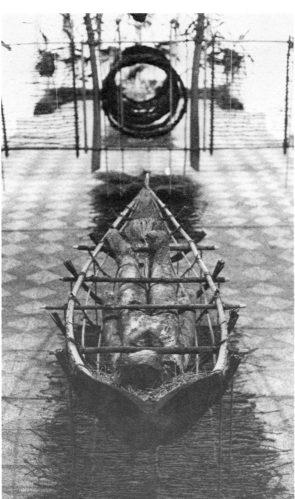

117

# JAN YATSKO

"The Return of Halley's Comet," wool, painted reed, cotton thread, ribbon, plastic cylinder, 7"x15", 1982. Photos of Jan Yatsko and her work by Scott Kriner.

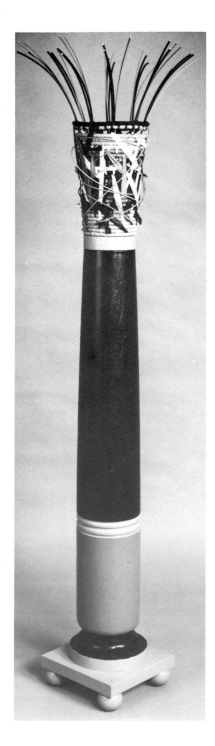

W hoever said "curiosity killed the cat" was just searching for a catchy phrase. That person didn't know cats and didn't know human nature!

There are several similarities between my creative experiences and a cat's behavior. Growing up as an only child, I learned to become comfortable with solitude and to think independently. Most of my childhood was spent finding within myself activities for a single participant. This continuous introspection enabled me to develop my own resources and to stimulate my own curious nature. My childhood experiences taught me that solitude, with good classical or jazz music in the background, gives the proper atmosphere in which to develop creative ideas and to carry them out.

Even as the cat sleeps, he is aware of the activity around him. My creative ideas are formulated through my own curiosity and my desire to interact with other creative individuals. The aura of mystery connected to the interior of a container fascinated me. The thought of what might be in the container, and the act of

finding out, inspired me to create my own irresistible containers. I made my first baskets in 1976, and my primary purpose was to produce well-constructed pieces. As my craftsmanship improved, I started to experiment with color and to stretch the limits of the coiling technique. The inclination to build upon previous experiences led me to expand my range of materials with each new basket. First, barks and vines were added to the wool basket structure; then with my "bird's nest" basket series, I began to select any material which would convey my idea. This process paralleled my choice of materials with a bird's random selection for its nest.

The bird's nest basket series is a continuing tribute to birds and their incredible capability to build nests that sometimes defy gravity, are well crafted, and are aesthetically good. Birds are truly the first basketmakers. The nest series led to a curiosity about bird behavior, and half a dozen bird feeders now fill my modest city backyard. Watching the birds is year-round entertainment for myself, my husband

Above: "Baobab Basket #2," tulip poplar bark strips, wool, 10½"x21½", 1980.
Left: "A New Direction," wool, linen, silk, white birch bark, plastic rods, 7½"x13½", 1981.
Opposite page, left: "Egyptian Nights," painted porch post, ripstop nylon, painted reed, 8"x4'8", 1985.
Opposite right: "For the Folks Back Home," bamboo, wool, leather, cotton thread, buttons, 9½"x11½", 1983.

121

Below: "Manhattan Loft,"
tulip poplar bark, bamboo,
wool, linen, buttons,
9½"x21", 1982.
Right: "Tree House," tulip
poplar bark, bamboo,
embroidery thread, plastic
screening, 18"x28", 1983.

and our three cats.

The nest series happened to coincide with a time of intense career and artistic reflection. After eight years of creating detailed pieces of sculpture, I was experiencing a decline in motivation. To counteract this, I began to work in brilliant colors, tried to find humor in my work and my life, and continued to create, but through different avenues. I felt it wasn't important which medium or technique I used as much as it was important to continue to create. My humor manifested itself in the bird's nest series. I thought of common bird nesting sites and interpreted them in a lighthearted way. A piece titled "Manhattan Loft" depicted a nest in the tall buildings of Manhattan, but it also referred to the artist's lofts in SoHo. Another basket entitled "A Nest for Big Bird" was five feet tall, and was constructed on site during a five-day craft show. When the basket was completed, I topped it with six colorful origami birds, each two feet long.

One of the avenues I pursued was banner commissions. I was attracted to the festive colors and to the airy qualities of the fabric I used. I continue to find satisfaction in my banner work, but it has also brought me back to baskets. Recently I have begun to coil with the ripstop fabric and to create banner environments around baskets. The banner environments were a natural creative progression. The result is that I can view one of my baskets as a part of a whole creative picture and not as a separate entity.

It is rather amusing that many of my interests begin with the letter "b": Baskets, banners, ballet, bicycling . . . chocolate, cats. Well . . . "c" does follow "b"! Besides, we have now come full circle to "cats" and their "curiosity" and a little curiosity never hurt anyone!

# BRYANT HOLSENBECK

I am an urban basketmaker with my roots in nature. I study the way nature creates: the way tree roots grow and how they intertwine, or how pine cones are shaped and how they sow their seeds.

Yet the materials I use for my work come from people as well as from nature. I figure that what we produce industrially is just an extension of the natural formation process. So I take materials that I find or buy—yellow plastic strapping tape which wraps newspapers, old bottle caps and buttons, as well as honeysuckle, seaweed and rattan—and I weave objects out of them.

When I start to make something, I feel that I am in conversation with the materials. My vocabulary is my specific weaving or painting technique. When I teach beginning basketry, I always tell students not to worry about what their first baskets will look like. The job with the first one is to learn the specific technique and to get used to the feel of the materials. The finished piece and the process of making it are what I think art is all about—taking materials and putting them together to make a

whole. Birds do it all the time, and they don't even have fingers.

I began making baskets while living on Nantucket Island, a place with a rich basketry heritage. I was struck by the fact that almost all baskets are made from natural materials, though it is hard to tell because of the evenness with which the fibers are processed, bleached and dyed.

Well, I thought, I can make baskets which are useful, but which still look like the natural materials they were made from. When baskets were first made, people were fighting to survive, trying to separate themselves from the harshness of their surroundings. Now, we are all finding a need to put nature back into our lives, to protect it and keep it with us. So I began making baskets, which were functional pieces with the natural textures left intact whenever possible.

I am making my living now making new shapes—integrating classic techniques and designs with modern and traditional methods. The first time I made a basket which differed from the standard of what I thought a basket ought to be, I was afraid

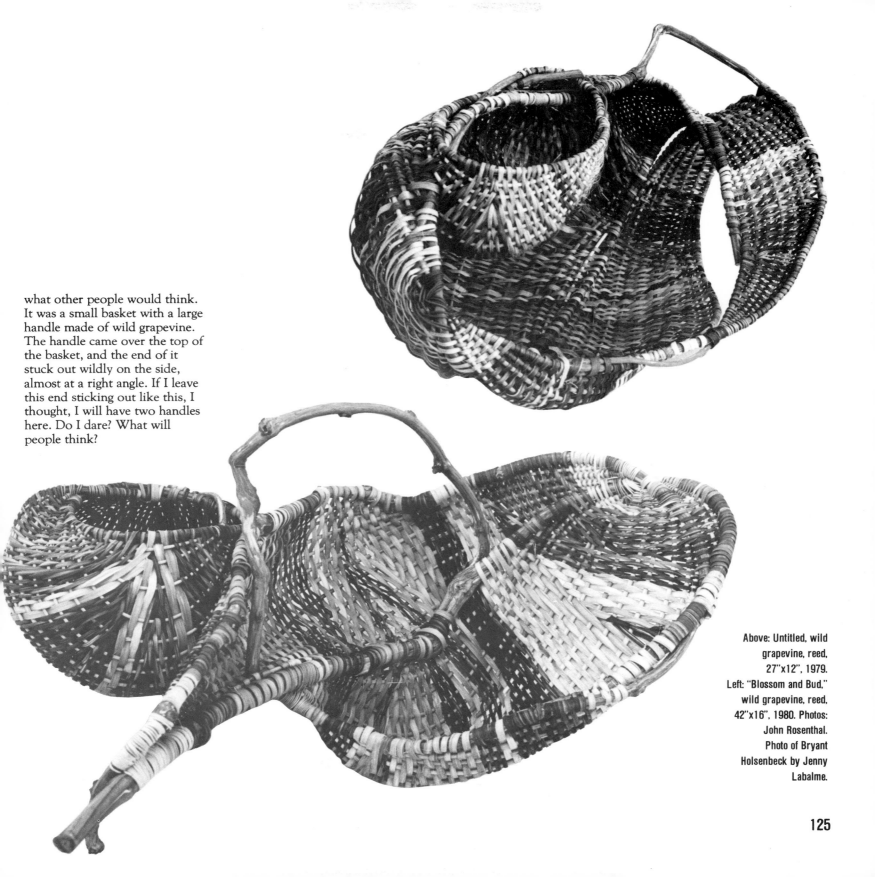

what other people would think. It was a small basket with a large handle made of wild grapevine. The handle came over the top of the basket, and the end of it stuck out wildly on the side, almost at a right angle. If I leave this end sticking out like this, I thought, I will have two handles here. Do I dare? What will people think?

Above: Untitled, wild grapevine, reed, 27"x12", 1979. Left: "Blossom and Bud," wild grapevine, reed, 42"x16", 1980. Photos: John Rosenthal. Photo of Bryant Holsenbeck by Jenny Labalme.

125

Because I was living on Nantucket, I had the opportunity to show my work with the Artist's Association there. I entered the basket in their summer show. To my great relief and delight, people were quite excited by it, and had a lot of fun with the two handles. It was a lesson in my own self-estimation and the opinions of others which I have never forgotten.

Over the years I have learned that my work is about change, about the evolution of form and ideas within the culture in which I live. Traditional techniques and materials are important evolutionary tools. I am learning that the choice for me is to take the risk, try as many new ideas as I can when they occur to me. And in the end, it has been good for business.

When I show my work, the two questions people most often ask me are number questions. How long, and how much? How long did it take me to do it? And how much does it cost?

These are practical questions. I have two answers I have worked up over the years concerning the how-long question. One of them is to tell them my

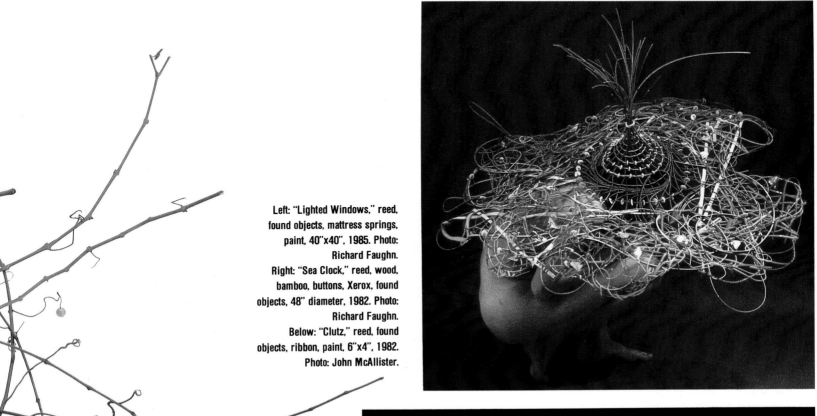

Left: "Lighted Windows," reed, found objects, mattress springs, paint, 40"x40", 1985. Photo: Richard Faughn.
Right: "Sea Clock," reed, wood, bamboo, buttons, Xerox, found objects, 48" diameter, 1982. Photo: Richard Faughn.
Below: "Clutz," reed, found objects, ribbon, paint, 6"x4", 1982. Photo: John McAllister.

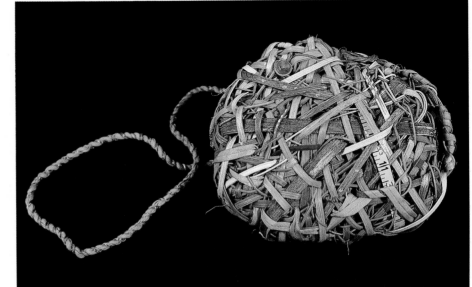

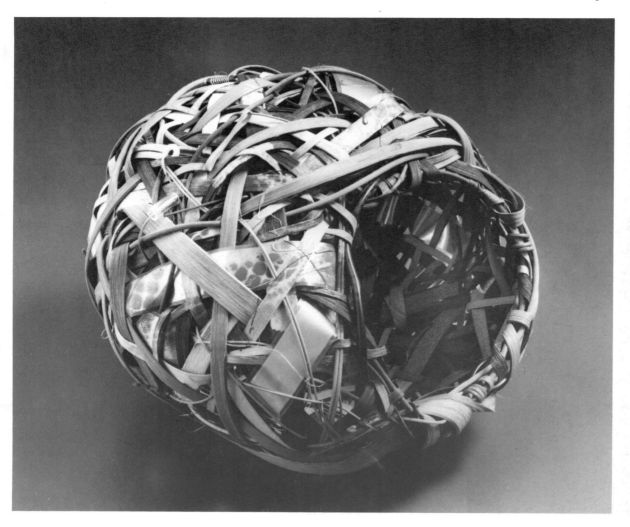

age, whatever it is, because my work has grown as I have grown. What I do now, I could not have done five years ago. It is experience layered upon experience which makes people ask this question. They sense that a great deal of learning has happened here.

The other answer is one an old tobacco farmer once gave me with a twinkle in his eye, when I asked him how long he worked each day. "Honey," he said, "if I knew I wouldn't do it." I know in a larger sense—say how much time each week I spend—how long my work takes to complete. But I drop time expectations while at work; that is the only way I can be truly involved.

I like to tell my students that baskets are about time. More than anything else, that's the value of them. They are not made from precious materials like gold of silver. There is no dramatic chemical transformation as in ceramics or metallurgy. There is simply time. There is the time spent gathering and processing the materials— whether you are stripping honeysuckle bark or unraveling telephone wire. And there is the time spent weaving—thread upon thread, twist and turn, twist and turn, until finally, the basket is complete. Finished. Ready to hold whatever you may choose. A finished basket is a mark of time spent. Within that is its value.

Sometimes people are surprised at how much my work costs, especially if they compare the prices of my baskets to the price of beautiful rattan weavings made, for example, in the Philippines, where people still get much less for their labor. We live in a world where we no longer need to make things by hand. We don't need baskets. After all, we have paper bags, plastic bags and cardboard boxes. Hand labor that was once necessary has been supplanted by mass production. Yet I feel that the creation and use of handmade things is of primary importance to our well-being. By understanding how something is made, we gain self-esteem, and a broader understanding of our place in the world. Expressing my ideas in what I make, and selling the finished work, is one way that I can communicate my understanding.

I find that what I have to say continues to expand. When I teach a class, my students always challenge me. I am forever seeing them do something that I didn't think could be done, or hadn't thought of before as a solution to a particular problem. I like to tell beginning students that they have the advantage of wide-open expectations. It is my job as an artist and a teacher to keep these expectations open, and to help them over the rough spots with techniques and encouragement. And I must constantly remind myself of the things I tell my students.

I have been weaving objects for almost a decade now. I see ahead of me risks that need taking—I need a new and larger studio, for instance, and need to expand my present work into still larger sculptures. If I think about how hard it will be I will remain where I am, with what I am already familiar with. But if I remember how important my own stepping ahead has been in the past, then the way is clearer. As an urban basketmaker, it seems that my job is to take the fabric of my past experience and keep weaving new possibilities.

129

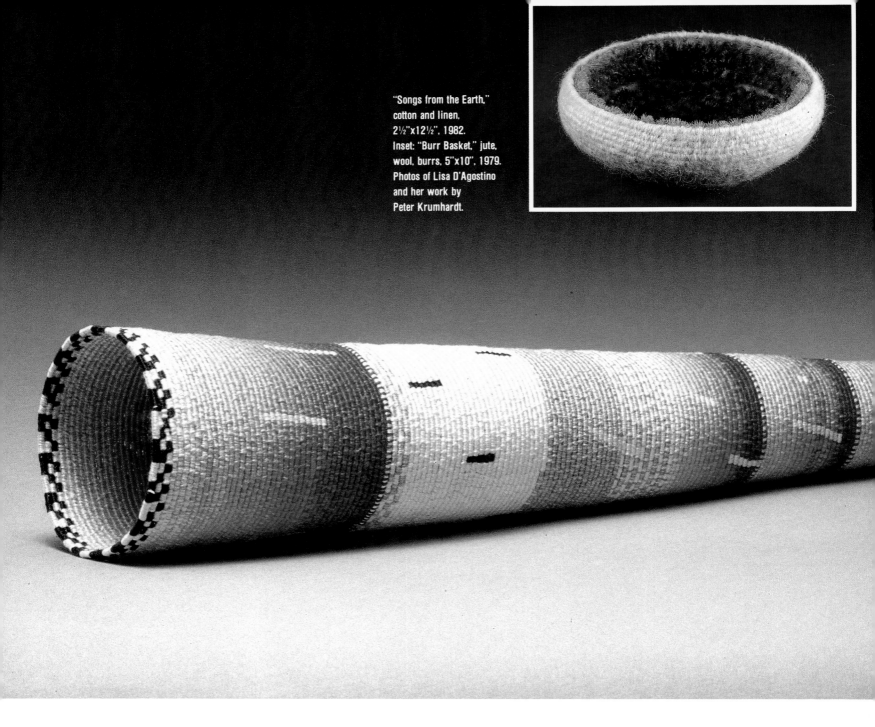

"Songs from the Earth,"
cotton and linen,
2½"x12½", 1982.
Inset: "Burr Basket," jute,
wool, burrs, 5"x10", 1979.
Photos of Lisa D'Agostino
and her work by
Peter Krumhardt.

# LISA D'AGOSTINO

Initially, I chose the coiling technique because of its convenience. I had the desire to do art work, but no money to buy materials. Coiling was attractive because it did not require a special studio or equipment. I could sit in my bedroom with a needle, scissors, yarns, and a card table to set it all on. Some of the yarns came from the local department store. Others were leftovers from fiber courses I took in college. The yarns were not all the best quality, but that was not a main concern at the time. My intention was to work and experiment with shapes and colors. The results were varied, but I learned what I liked and didn't like and had new ideas as I continued to work. I liked the tactile, rigid quality of the coiling. To focus on this quality, I kept the forms of the baskets simple. The form I fell in love with is the cone. It seems to echo the shape of towers and monuments that have been erected by many cultures for thousands of years. Mayan, Aztec and Egyptian pyramids have always fascinated me with their history, their purpose and their mystery. I began to use cotton embroidery

"The Wanderers: Mars, Earth, Venus," linen, cotton, 2½"x5½", 1983.

floss as wrapping material. It is available in hundreds of colors. I kept the baskets neutral in color.

About seven years ago I moved to Iowa. For most of this time I lived on several acres in the country. The view from the house was open sky and land, and in some ways they have become part of my work. It was a very calm place, and enabled me to work with the tedious technique of coiling with the embroidery floss. I think it also had a somewhat spiritual effect on me. Since living there, I have had a craving to visit vast, open places like those in the West and Southwest.

Soon after I moved to Iowa a friend reintroduced me to astronomy. I say "reintroduced" because my father explained the stars to me years ago, and sparked an interest that has lasted. I was hooked on astronomy for several years. I bought a star chart, telescope, astronomy books and magazines, joined an amateur astronomy club, and went to a few "star parties." I spent a lot of time reading about astronomy, and spent hours outside at night learning the constellations and the locations of var-

ious stars. I was amazed that I could see the rings of Saturn and the four moons of Jupiter right from my backyard. I loved it, and its influence appeared immediately in the baskets. The places and events in the baskets have astronomical themes, as do all the titles. Some of the inspiration has come from magazine articles, the "Cosmos" television series, a billboard along the

133

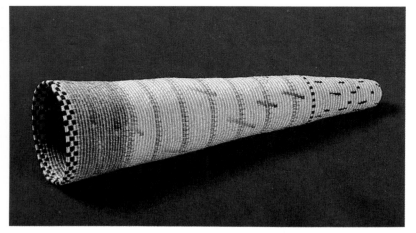

highway in Arizona, and current events.

While astronomy was working its influence, color slowly appeared. At first it was only little bits of complementary color with neutrals of black, gray and white. It didn't seem possible to work with many different colors and all the strands of cotton without going crazy. I started with a little color and slowly worked up to more complicated patterns, with more color in each new piece. I graded the colors from light to dark, usually on a neutral background. Eventually, I began to use graded color in the foreground and background as well.

With so many color gradations, the embroidery floss has to be organized in some way. I use three strands of floss. They might be three different colors, or two strands might be the same color and the third strand a shade or two lighter or darker. I arrange rows of these combinations from light to dark on heavy paper. Then I tape them down and number them. The color gradations are subtle, so it is important to number everything. When one color combination

"Welcome to Meteor City,"
linen, cotton, 2½"x5½"
each, 1984.

runs out it is easy to determine what is needed.

The process of coiling, with so many strands of color coming and going, is very slow. Working once around a five-inch circumference can take an hour, and completing one inch of coiling can take eight hours. It takes a lot of time but time is always a problem anyway. I work full time, and the only time for art work is in the evenings or on weekends. Most of the artists I know seem to have problems similar to this. Luckily, most of my summers have been free and they provide the only large blocks of time in which to work.

Accomplishing art work while holding a full-time job has made life hectic at times, as well as frustrating. When I am at my job, my thoughts continually turn to the baskets and what I could be doing, or what I want to do next. While I'm working on a basket, thoughts of the job sneak in and I wish I didn't have to go to work tomorrow. It's a double life! Overall, it has worked out pretty well. The important thing is to *make* the time to work, and to use that time in the best possible way.

"Welcome to Meteor City,"
linen, cotton, 2½"x5½"
each, 1984.

# RACHEL NASH LAW

In 1985 my husband and I moved back to West Virginia after an absence of seven years. We both felt a need for the mountains, a more familiar environment and a place to settle down. The move has made such a difference! I have become a morning worker, excited about the quiet and the long stretch of time in the day that seems to come with an early rising. I feel that the serenity of these mountain surroundings and the richness of their basketry materials will eventually influence my work.

For the past four years I have been interviewing traditional basketmakers in conjunction with a writing project. Seeing so many different baskets and the details of their construction has shown me a whole new variety of technical features. This study has begun to manifest itself in my own baskets. The biggest influence on my work comes from three historical types of white oak baskets: the rib basket, made with a framework and ribs; the split basket, mainly made with flat weaving materials; and the rod basket, made with a round white oak rod woven in a

variety of wickerwork forms. These baskets, along with the original purpose of baskets—practical containers for storage or transportation—are the inspiration for my work at this time.

I have worked with many materials, including bark, vines, and shoots, but I prefer white oak as my basketry material. Working with white oak in basketry is like working green wood, and requires a variety of tools and technical skills. White oak is a very elastic and pliable wood, and lends itself to many different basket forms. White oak is strong and durable, but lightweight and easy to maintain. The work itself is clean work, surrounded by fresh smells. The shavings are easy to sweep up and are used either as fire starter or in the garden as mulch.

A suitable white oak tree is not easy to find. It must be a young tree and free of blemishes or disease. The trunk must be straight, six to eight inches in diameter. Sometimes it takes the better part of the day to find good timber, but the ease in preparation and the beauty of the wood make the search for the right tree worthwhile. My

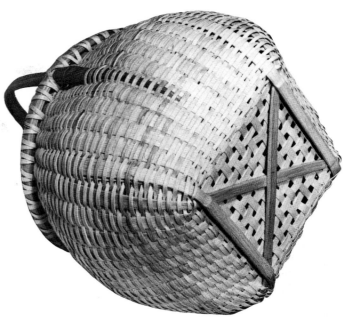

Below: Stacked hoop basket #2, white oak rib, 8"x14", 1985.
Right: Footed split basket, white oak, 11¾"x15¾", 1985.

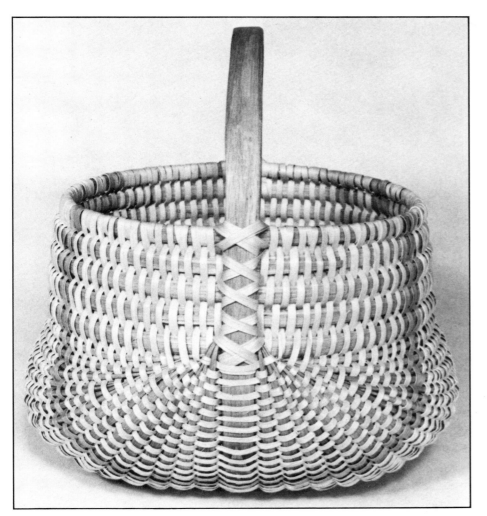

Left: Hamper, white oak, 24"x16", 1984.
Above left: Round lidded basket, white oak, 9¼"x19", 1985.
Above right: Basket skeleton, white oak, hickory bark, doweling, 12"x19", 1984.

husband helps with the search and with the physical labor of cutting and hauling the log out of the woods. He sometimes does the initial splitting of the log, dividing it into quarters, but I do the rest in order to get the exact size and shape I want.

Preparation of material and the actual basketmaking cannot be separated. Usually I have an idea of what I would like to make, but try to leave the form open for change, in case a better idea should surface, or the materials seem better suited to something else.

There is something new to learn on each piece of work. Each tree handles a bit differently, and some make better basket material. Much of the work depends on the tree's pliability and how it meets the needs of a particular basket. In addition to the wood itself, construction techniques often become strong design elements and act differently with different basket forms. Varying and combining techniques in different types of baskets leads to the creation of new forms and new ideas.

For the past six years most of my work has been on a small production line, and I've made an occasional exhibition basket as needed. That work method now seems to be completely reversed, with more time spent on experimental and exhibition pieces than for production items. I feel that I am finally to the place where I can go ahead and work through a series with a single construction feature or a basket form as the idea base. The apprenticeship is over, but the commitment to the craft remains, and the search for ideas is definitely still in progress.

Right: Lidded willow basket, 10"x9½", 1979.
Below right: Single-V gathering basket, white oak, 17"x14", 1985.
Center page: Round rod and split basket, white oak, 17"x14", 1985.

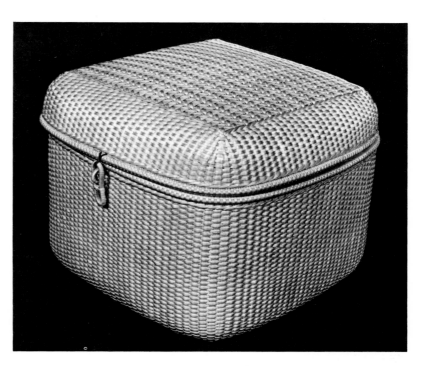

# SHEREEN LaPLANTZ

**M**y baskets are an interaction of form and texture. They're an extension of the things I love, functioning one at a time, then in conjunction.

The above statement is the result of a lengthy discovery process. I have a thorough art background, as a weaver. I began studying art in junior high school and continued through graduate school. I learned that I wanted to be *good* as an artist. Being bad would have been okay, too; at least that could have been done with flair. What I feared was mediocrity—I knew I had to develop a solid technical background, an understanding of what I liked, why, and how to achieve it. I was patient, and clocked a great deal of time in the studio. Fortunately, I finally got tired of waiting and began to do only what I wanted to do—baskets.

Three elements have surfaced in my work and have become recurring themes: texture, architecture (I continually explore shapes), and layering. Each element has developed in each of my recent styles. And I do like a technical challenge. When a

technique becomes too easy for me, I branch off into another style.

My first baskets were simply an exploration of textures. I used a form with straight sides, a square base, and a round top. I embellished it with surface curls in every way I could imagine. I made hundreds of these, and developed an intimacy with basketry. It was working on these curled baskets that hooked me, that finally lured me away from weaving and into basketry. It was also during this time that I developed my understanding of what a basket is, what sizes and proportions I like, and how I want to work with materials. The textural surface curls were no longer enough, and I became concerned with shapes.

I continued to play with textures, and tried thatching—like thatched roofs. The baskets, as extensions of me, became ladies, and I dressed them. Sometimes it felt like I was playing with dolls, but more often it related to the fashion history which I enjoy reading. I made hundreds of the thatched ladies, and learned that I don't like texture for texture's sake alone. No matter how much

I like it, that one design element can't overwhelm the object. This style let me understand how I feel about texture, how much of it I want on a piece, how closely it should hug the object, and that it needs to work in conjunction with my other themes. I like

those ladies, even now.

After the ladies, I no longer worked with just one design element at a time. Textures continue to be a primary concern in my work. And they are becoming more elaborate. They've become another layer of basket, or a network covering the surface, or even other baskets worked on the surface of the base basket. In my dreams I honeycomb the surfaces of my baskets with textures.

The second recurring element in my basketry is architecture. It actually started as shaping. I became bored with simple, basic forms and began to try more involved shapes. At first

**Opposite: Untitled pyramid, flat paper, fiber splint, reed, waxed linen, 12"x9", 1981. Photo of Shereen LaPlantz by David LaPlantz.**

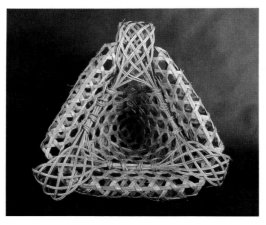

Left: Untitled double layer basket, flat and round reed, 15"x12", 1985.
Below: Untitled pyramid, flat paper, fiber splint, lauhala, waxed linen, 10"x10", 1981.
Opposite: Untitled double layer basket, flat and round reed, splint, 28"x23", 1983.

these were influenced by other baskets, primarily from Southeast Asia and the Philippines.

Then I began to work with pyramids. These were far more complex shapes, and didn't even *feel* like baskets. They were a direct response to architecture. These baskets looked like skylines, like contemporary buildings, or like a hillside covered with small houses. Through these baskets I was finally able to combine texture with a complex shape.

Shaping hasn't been a primary concern since I made the pyramids. Now it's simply part of the way I view a new technique. It's also an element that *must* be in my basketry. Like a "given" in math, it's automatically there to build on. When I find a new material, when I'm depressed and just want to make baskets, or when I feel dry, I play with shapes. Shapes are fun. They're also spontaneous. I might be working on one idea, and halfway through another presents itself, already finished. Shaping demands that I keep a fresh eye. Expecting to see only one thing eliminates all the discoveries along the way. And it's

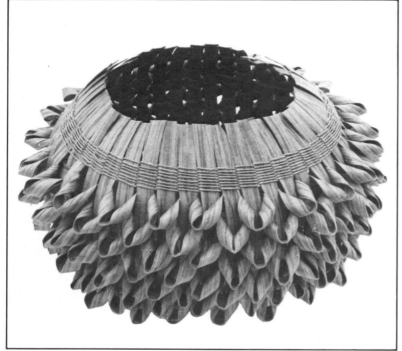

those discoveries that create the forms for my basketry.

The final element in my basketry is layering. This is almost texture, and its result is surface texture, but it's based on clothing. While dressing the thatched ladies I did some layering, with overskirts and aprons and head scarves. The thought of layering one thing over another kept nagging at me. I had tried some openwork baskets, but they were too open, a bit formless, and far too fragile. The obvious solution was to put the lace basket over a solid form, another basket.

This form is still fascinating to me. It has evolved through several styles. First I made openwork round reed baskets over some of my favorite solid forms. These were baskets I made for me: they didn't photograph well, so I couldn't get them in print. Next I tried openwork with openwork, which allowed me to have two baskets intersect, to actually weave in and out of each other. They didn't even have to be the same shape. I learned to think of two layers, two separate baskets as a single unit, a single skin that could be applied to another solid

form. Since at least one of the openwork layers was always hexagonal plaiting, I also learned to think of weaving in three directions at once. Then there was the big breakthrough, when I learned that three-directional plaiting can be shaped the same as regular plaiting. What I knew about shaping would transfer. I could continue to play with shapes, but play with them in the current technique.

Finally I learned that mad weave, another three-directional weave, is a cousin of hexagonal plaiting. One is the open form, the other is solid. They mesh together. They cooperate so that hexagonal plaiting can flow over and tuck into the surface of mad weave. I've only begun to play with mad weave, and don't yet know what it has to offer me. But it sounds like a technique that's made to suit all my interests, as it fascinates me as much as each of the styles before it did.

With each new style I go through a specific process. I find that a technical problem has been fascinating me for a long time. First it sort of nags, then it arouses curiosity, causing me to dabble and be frustrated, finally

Below: Untitled double layer basket, flat and round reed, splint, 11"x8", 1983.
Opposite top: Untitled thatched lady, reed, raffia, palm bark, 12"x7", 1979.
Opposite bottom: Untitled, paper, fiber, splint, waxed linen, 14"x7", 1978.

it demands full attention. I learn the new technique through simple basic forms. When I was a beginning basketmaker I would then embellish the simple forms with texture. Now I make, in the new weave, some of the more complex shapes I enjoy, then add the textures. Working on surface texture helps me understand a technique. Through adding embellishment I learn what's happening with the technique; how it's shaped, what the rules are and which can be broken, and what numbers of elements work best for the things I try. This is when I learn to like the technique. Once I understand the technique, I start to work on shaping. When I can control the shape, and have developed the complexity I want, then I either compound or layer. To "compound" is to build a basket on top or on the side of a basket. It's at this point that the baskets come alive, develop personality, and become magical.

I make my baskets because I like them. It takes tons of perseverance and discipline to get them to a point where you might like them too. And it's worth every minute.

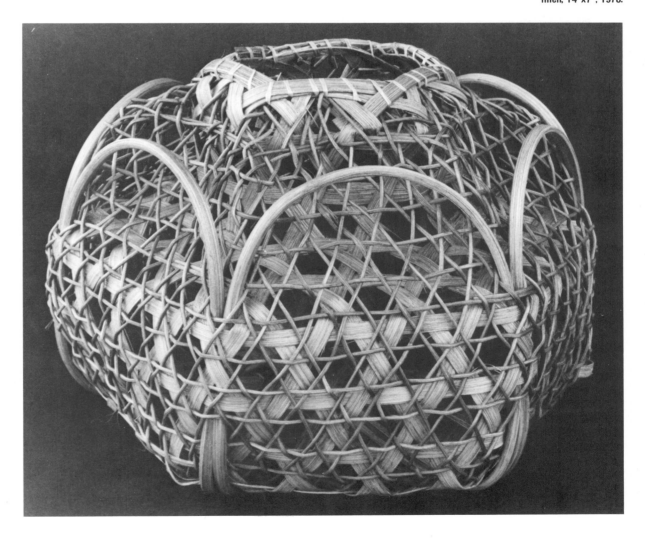

145

# NANCY MOORE BESS

T en years ago, I was concerned about mastering the traditional basketry techniques in the purest forms and in using those techniques to create containers. Everything was quite clear and linear. I taught a great deal and wrote a number of articles. But research into the cross-cultural aspects of basketry led me to realize basketry techniques, and related fiber techniques, had much broader application than I had realized.

I started reading books like *Shelter*, *The Houses of Mankind* and *Craftsmen of Necessity* and was fascinated to find wickerwork and plaiting used on the

Opposite: "Temporary Basket," natural raffia, 9½"x6", 1984. Photo: Doug Long. Photo of Nancy Moore Bess by Bob Hanson.

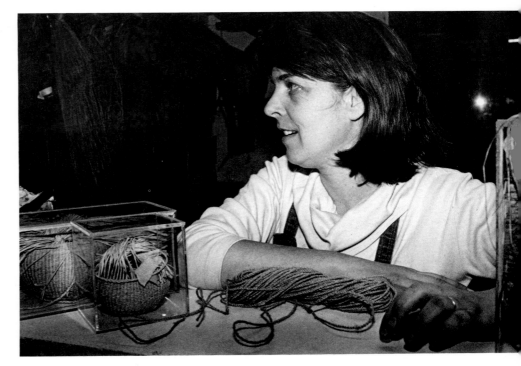

sides of homes, bamboo used for scaffolding, wicker techniques in the wattle fencing of England. I began collecting fans and brooms that incorporated basketry techniques, and I looked to the Pacific Basin area for further inspiration. A study of this region's techniques led me to the use of ropes and cordage: coir (coconut fiber), nawa palm, manila, and sisal. Ropes led me to dyeing, not because of a commitment to natural dyes, but because of a desire to control color and because coir and manila take color so well. Financial considerations led me to raffia, which I now consider my perfect material.

What began as a single focal point—basketry—became instead the core from which many other interests branch. Work developed, not singularly, but rather in related series. Increasingly, my work reflects my ongoing interest in fencing, screens, dwellings, fiber armor and thatching.

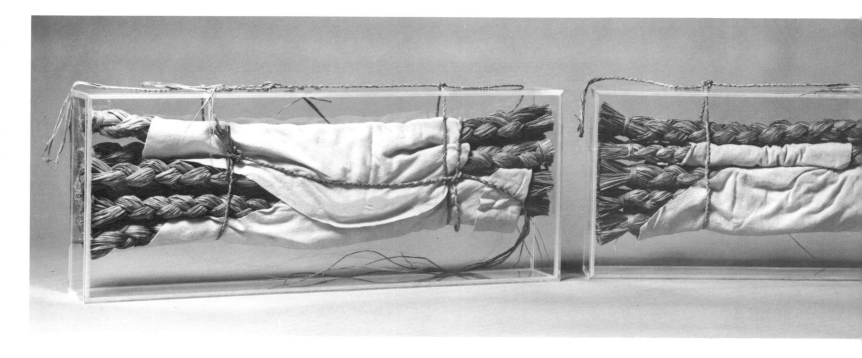

Opposite top: From "With a Nod to Japan" series, natural raffia, 4½"x4½", 1984. Opposite bottom: "Chamois Bundle," hand-dyed raffia, natural chamois, 22"x9", 1984-85. Photos: Bob Hanson. Top, this page: "Pink Palm Bundle," hand-dyed raffia, palm leaves, 22"x9", 1984. Bottom, this page: "Volcanic Ash," paper, 3"x4½", 1977. Photo: Bob Hanson.

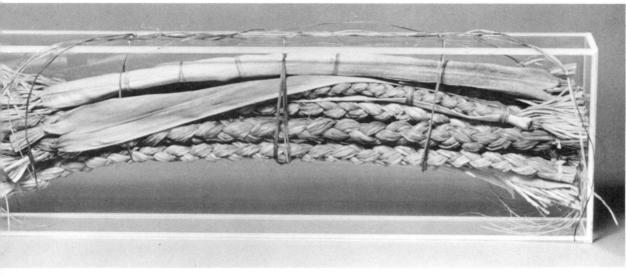

My current research style is a combination of "good ol' librarian" (that is what I did with my B.A.), clipping and recording, plus what I affectionately call "mental cataloging." It took years of looking at fiber armor before "Private Armor" and subsequent pieces evolved. What a sense of satisfaction when it came together!

I have no interest in trying to predict what will evolve in my work, but hope, instead, that I can remain flexible—something that doesn't come easily for me. I will finish the wattle fencing behind my herb garden and my perennial bed in Connecticut. I will continue to learn about bamboo until I can grow it myself and prepare it for basketry.

While doing these wonderful things, I will also iron my pillowcases (because I can't stand them wrinkled), hang my laundry out on the line whenever possible, have lots of animals around, read mysteries, buy old table linens at yard sales, cook the things my family loves while teaching them to love cumin as much as I do, be involved in peace projects, and share my energy with those I care for. Why? Because one doesn't work in isolation. Basketry is *part* of my life . . . not my life.

No more time to write. Back to the studio. I want to re-dye some reed for a new project and must meet Ivan's bus at three. It is raining, the cat, Grape Nuts, must now get off my lap, and I must say ENOUGH.

Left: "Post Modern Taos," hand-dyed rattan reed, corn husks, raffia, 17"x11", 1985-86. Photo: Bob Hanson.

Right: Untitled pair, dyed coir rope, hand-painted manila rope, 28" diameter. Photo: Doug Long.

Below: From "With a Nod to Japan" series, natural raffia, chamois, 5"x5", 1984-85. Photo: Doug Long.

# JOHN MCQUEEN

T
he baskets I make are branches of trees rearranged and no longer real the way a tree is real. Yet, for the moment they are themselves and they carry their intent. Though they will straighten and release their uncertainty, they are now corners and condense what is around them. They are an organization bent on isolation; a rationalization for changes in nature wrapped around a hole. It is this hold, this insisting, this fortification held against momentum that these sticks guard against. It is an outside needing its inside. An obsession strong enough to change them from what they are into what they do. These are branches of trees arranged and unreal and for the moment they are having themselves.

Untitled basket, ash, grapevine, paint, 11"x25", 1985. Photo: Brian Oglesbee, courtesy of Bellas Artes Gallery. Photo of John McQueen by Jessie Shefrin.

moss, 10"x11", 1977.
Bottom right: Untitled
basket, basswood, pine
bark, 15"x17", 1986.
Photo: Brian Oglesbee,
courtesy of Nina
Freudenheim Gallery.
Below: Untitled basket,
raspberry canes, red osier,
9"x32", 1985. Photo: Brian
Oglesbee, courtesy of
Bellas Artes Gallery.

Opposite: Untitled baskets,
bark, wood, 18"x20",
1984. Photo: Brian
Oglesbee, courtesy of Nina
Freudenheim Gallery.
Top right: Untitled basket,
malaluka bark, Spanish

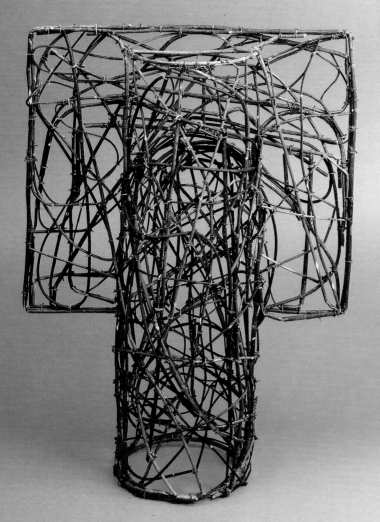

Top left: Untitled basket, white pine bark, 8"x18", 1977. Photo: Lester Mertz.
Below right: Untitled basket, day lily stalks, willow bark, 13"x15", 1980. Photo: Stephen Myers.
Below left: Untitled basket, birch bark, 13"x14", 1978.

# DONA LOOK

M y work with white birch bark began with an interest in the folded bark containers made by the Woodland Indians. These single-fiber baskets were constructed with minimal shaping and altera-tion of materials. I started weav-ing strips of handmade paper into small containers, and strips of birch bark into sheets to be used like fabric. Eventually,

Clockwise, from above:
Untitled, white birch bark,
waxed silk, 5½"x8½",
1985. Photo: Sanderson
Photography. Untitled,
white birch bark, waxed
linen, silk, 8"x9", 1984.
Photo: Ralph Gabriner.
Untitled, white birch bark,
waxed silk, 7½"x8¾",
1985. Photo: Sanderson
Photography. "Fish

Strainer," white birch
bark, waxed linen, 20"x7".
1983. Photo: Ralph
Gabriner.
Photo of Dona Look by
Ken Loeber.

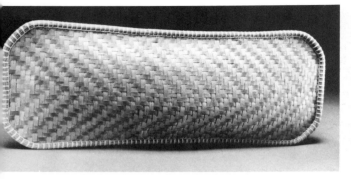

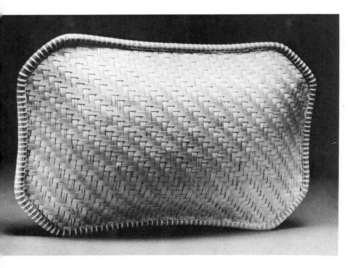

Top: "Derr Pillow," white birch bark, waxed linen, balsam needles, grass, 20¼"x3", 1983.
Bottom: "Tré Pillow," white birch bark, waxed linen, balsam needles, grass, 16¼"x3", 1983.
Center: Untitled three, white birch bark, waxed linen, silk. Photos: Sanderson Photography.

birch bark took the place of the handmade paper. Although I continue to experiment with other materials native to northern Wisconsin (cedar bark, black ash, willow), my present concern is exploring the use of white birch both in sheet and strip form.

Since the trees have individual characteristics, each piece of bark is unique. Often the process of gathering, sorting, and preparing the bark dictates appropriate use of the materials. A common element to emerge in this work is the juxtaposition of a consistent woven pattern with the irregular natural lines on the sheets of bark.

I consciously limit the techniques and materials I employ so that I can concentrate on form. I think of these pieces as vessels rather than baskets since practical function is of little interest to me. I minimize decorative elements, but the use of silk thread allows me to add subtle lines of color. I find the decorative qualities are inherent in the materials. While the resulting vessels are measured and monochromatic, I feel the essence of my work is in the forms and simplicity of construction.

161

**NANCY MOORE BESS**, New York, NY

Nancy Moore Bess earned a B.A. from the University of California-Davis, and studied at the State University of New York at Stony Brook, Columbia University, and the Fashion Institute of Technology.

Exhibitions of Bess' work include Works in Miniature at Elements, Greenwich, Connecticut; Basketry, Gallery North, Setauket, New York; and traveling exhibits, The New Basket: A Vessel for the Future, and Texture, Form and Style in the Marketplace.

Her work has appeared in *Contemporary Basketry*, *House and Garden*, *Fiberarts* magazine, *Craft Australia*, and she wrote the book *Step-by-Step Basketry* (Golden Press).

Bess is a member of the New York Textile Study Group, an association of nearly 50 artists who share a common interest in the fiber arts.

**JOANNE SEGAL BRANDFORD**, 200 Brookfield Road, Ithaca, NY 14850

Joanne Segal Brandford has exhibited widely, with solo shows in New York, California, and New Jersey. Group exhibits since 1975 include Fiberworks, the Tyler School of Art group invitational exhibition; In the Spirit of the Inca, Berkeley, California; IV Textile Triennale, Lodz, Poland; The New Basket: A Vessel for the Future, Brainerd Art Gallery, Potsdam, New York; Basketry Now, Lawton Gallery, Green Bay, Wisconsin; and After Her Own Image: Woman's Work 1985, Winston-Salem, North Carolina.

In 1986, Brandford had two-person shows at 15 Steps Gallery in Ithaca, New York, and at Swain School of Design in New Bedford, Massachusetts.

*Ms.* magazine, *The Village Voice*, *Fiberarts* magazine, *Craft Horizons*, *The Boston Globe*, and *AIA Journal* are among the publications which have featured her work, which also has appeared in several books, including *Textile Art* (Rizzoli), *The New Basketry* (Van Nostrand Reinhold), and *Weaving Off-Loom* (Regnery).

Brandford earned a B.A. in decorative art and an M.A. in design from the University of California at Berkeley. She has been a member of Amos Eno Gallery, New York, since 1977.

**JAN BUCKMAN**

Jan Buckman was a 1985 fellowship recipient from Arts Midwest and the National Endowment for the Arts. She studied basketry and rugs on the Navajo and Hopi Reservations in Arizona.

Group shows in which her work has appeared include Baskets and Quilts in Philadelphia; New Wisconsin Fiber, Lausanne, Switzerland; Fine Focus in St. Louis; ArtQuest '85, a traveling exhibit; and Basketry Today, organized by the University of Wisconsin.

**LISA D'AGOSTINO**

Lisa D'Agostino earned a B.F.A. from Bowling Green State University, and she works both in fiber and in metal. Invitational exhibits in which her work was shown include Fiber Miniatures, The Hand and The Spirit Gallery, Scottsdale, Arizona; Fine Focus, Craft Alliance Gallery, St. Louis; Northwest Southwest Influence, Sarah Squeri Gallery, Cincinnati; The Basketry Link, Mendocino (California) Art Center, and Fiber National '84, Dunkirk, New York. Her work has appeared in several books, including *Jewelry—Contemporary Design and Technique* (Davis) and *Jewelry—Basic Techniques and Design* (Chilton), and in a number of magazine articles as well.

**MICHAEL DAVIS**, 3520 Herschel Street, Jacksonville, FL 32205

Michael Davis studied painting, ceramics, graphic design, sculpture, printmaking, spinning, dyeing, and weaving while earning a B.A. from the University of North Florida.

His first solo show was in 1980, Jacksonville, Florida, and he has exhibited since then in group shows throughout the United States. His work has appeared in several publications, including *Fiberarts* magazine and *Shuttle Spindle & Dyepot*.

Davis has taught at the Brookfield (Connecticut) Craft Center, the Jacksonville (Florida) Art Museum, and at The Florida Tropical Weavers Guild State Convention.

**LILLIAN ELLIOTT**, 1775 San Lorenzo, Berkeley, CA 94707

Upon receiving an M.F.A. from Cranbrook Academy of Art, Lillian Elliott became a fabric designer for the Ford Motor Company. She has lectured and instructed since 1959, most recently at San Francisco Community College and at the Conference of Northern California Handweavers. Elliott has juried the Craftsmen's Association of British Columbia Exhibition, the San Francisco Art Festival, San Mateo County Arts Council Textile Exhibit, and the Marin Society of Artists 57th Annual Show.

Her work has appeared in many invitational shows, including Contemporary American Basket-Makers, Purdue University; Woven Structures, London; and Vannerie, Museum of Decorative Arts, Lausanne, Switzerland. She has had more than a dozen solo shows, and has exhibited at the Twelfth Tapestry Biennial in Lausanne. Since 1981 she has collaborated with textile artist Pat Hickman; their works have shown throughout the United States and in Europe and Japan.

Articles about Elliott and her work have been published in *Handweaver's Bulletin*, *The Goodfellow Review of Crafts*, *Fiberarts* magazine, and *American Craft*. Her work has appeared in *Ms.*, *Craft Horizons*, *The San Francisco Examiner*, *Artweek*, and in more than 20 books. She has written for *American Craft*, *Arts and Activities*, and *Minnesota Weaver Quarterly*.

In 1985 Elliott received a travel grant from the Swedish Women's Educational Association International. That same year she was designated a California Living Treasure.

**DOUGLAS ERIC FUCHS**

Doug Fuchs earned degrees from Catholic University and Columbia University, and for ten years was a Christian Brother. He taught weaving and basketry in school and museum art programs.

Fuchs' work has shown at galleries throughout the country, including The Elements Gallery, Greenwich, Connecticut; The Artisans Gallery, New York; the Following Sea Gallery, Hawaii. His work has been featured in such publications as *Fiberarts* magazine and *Shuttle Spindle & Dyepot*.

A major installation, "Floating Forest," commissioned by the Crafts Council of Australia, was mounted in Adelaide, Melbourne, and Sydney to high critical acclaim. Fuchs also received a fellowship from the National Endowment for the Arts.

Doug Fuchs died as this book was being prepared.

**JOHN GARRETT**, 3212 Larissa Drive, Los Angeles, CA 90026

John Garrett has taught at several California colleges and at the Kansas City Art Institute. He currently is on the faculty at the University of California at Los Angeles. His exhibitions include Master Fiber Works, Kansas City, Missouri; Works in Miniature, New York; L.A.V.A. '81, Los Angeles; Basketry: Tradition in New Form, Boston; Fiber Miniatures, Scottsdale, Arizona; the Vehta Biennale, Brussels; The Art of Basketry, Louisville, Kentucky; California Basketry: Past and Present, San Diego, California; Fiber R/Evolution, Milwaukee, Wisconsin; Woven Works, University of Wisconsin; and Basketry: Tradition in New Form, Boston and New York.

Garrett has completed collaborative work with Neda Al-Hilali, Marilyn Anderson, and Mary Ann Glantz. He has traveled throughout Europe and to Ghana and Afghanistan. In 1983, he won a National Endowment for the Arts fellowship, and in 1984 completed a 16-by-40-foot mural on Santa Monica Boulevard in Hollywood.

**MARIAN HAIGH-NEAL**, 2600 Bridle Path, Austin, TX 78703

Marian Haigh-Neal studied at Kansas State University, then received her B.F.A. from Arkansas State University. She lectured to graduate students and faculty at The Royal College of Art, London, and in 1980 won a grant from the Texas Commission on the Arts to serve in the Arts in Schools program. Haigh-Neal's work has appeared in exhibits throughout the country, and articles about her work have been published by *Fiberarts* magazine, *American Craft*, and *Metropolis*.

**BRYANT HOLSENBECK**, Durham, NC

After earning an M.Ed. from the University of North Carolina-Chapel Hill in 1972, Bryant Holsenbeck worked in the citrus groves of Kibbutz Evron in Israel. She then attended workshops at Penland School, Arrowmont School of Crafts, and Alfred University.

Her work has appeared in Contemporary Basketry, Gatlinburg, Tennessee; Crafts Invitational at the Southeastern Center for Contemporary Art; National Invitational, The Art of Adornment, American Crafts in Iceland, National Basketry Invitational, Louisville, Kentucky; U.S.A.—Portrait of the South, Rome, Italy; Fiber Sculpture at the Green Hill Center for North Carolina Art; National Basketry Invitational, Brookfield (Connecticut) Craft Center; and Basketry Invitational, Kohler Arts Center, Sheboygan, Wisconsin.

Holsenbeck taught at workshops at the Greenville County (South Carolina) Museum of Art, Penland School, and the Haystack Mountain School of Crafts, and was a visiting artist in the Virginia school system.

In 1985 she received an Emerging Artist grant from the Durham (North Carolina) Arts Council. In 1986, Holsenbeck mounted a solo show at The Private Collection gallery, Cincinnati.

## LISSA HUNTER, 89 Mackworth Street, Portland, ME 04103

Lissa Hunter's works are in several corporate collections. She has had solo and two-person exhibits from Maine to New Mexico, and has been included in group shows such as Fiber Forms 1979, Nashua, New Hampshire; Miniatures, Cannon Beach, Oregon; Within and Beyond the Basket, Berkeley, California; and Winter Artists, Taos, New Mexico. Hunter's work has shown at Clay and Fiber Gallery in Taos, New Mexico, Netsky Gallery in Coconut Grove, Florida, Gallery on the Green in Lexington, Massachusetts, and the Elaine Horwitch Gallery in Scottsdale, Arizona.

Hunter holds a B.A. in fine arts and an M.F.A. in textile arts from Indiana University.

## FERNE JACOBS

Ferne Jacobs studied painting and weaving, and earned an M.F.A. from Claremont Graduate School. Exhibitions of her fiber work, drawings, and basketry include First World Crafts Exhibition, Toronto; First International Exhibition of Miniature Textiles, London; The Basket-maker's Art, New York; The Contemporary Basketmaker, Purdue University; Beyond Tradition: 25th Anniversary Exhibition of the American Craft Museum, New York; American Basket Forms, Brookfield (Connecticut) Craft Center; Poetry of the Physical, American Craft Museum; Fiber R/Evolution, Milwaukee; Fibre Structures, The Denver Art Museum; and Fiberworks, an international invitational fibers exhibition, the Cleveland Museum of Art.

Her work has been featured in a number of magazines, including Artweek, American Craft, Craft Horizons, and Fiberarts; and in books, such as A Modern Approach to Basketry, In Praise of Hands: Contemporary Crafts of the World (New York Graphic Society), Beyond Weaving (Watson-Guptill), and The Art Fabric: Mainstream (Van Nostrand Reinhold).

Jacobs has lectured throughout the United States, most recently at Rhode Island School of Design, Tyler School of Art, Philadelphia School of Art, and the University of Wisconsin. She has received two grants from the National Endowment for the Arts. Her work is included in a number of private and public collections.

## SHEREEN LAPLANTZ, 899 Bayside Cutoff, Bayside, CA 95524

Shereen LaPlantz began her career as a weaver. She holds a B.A. from California State University at Los Angeles, and studied design at Cranbrook Academy of Art, Bloomfield Hills, Michigan.

She has written and published two books, The Mad Weave Book and Plaited Basketry: The Woven Form. She publishes The News Basket, and her work has appeared in The New York Times, Fiberarts magazine, Craft Australia, and The Washington Post. LaPlantz has exhibited widely in group and solo shows, including those at the Pacific Basin School of Textile Arts; Brookfield (Connecticut) Craft Center; the 1982 Convergence exhibit in Seattle; the History Museum in Gdansk, Poland; Mendocino Arts Center, California; and D W Gallery, Dallas.

She studied Maori fiber techniques in New Zealand, Aboriginal basketry in Australia, and participated in a workshop with the Akwesasne basketmakers on the Mohawk reservation in Hogansburg, New York.

## RACHEL NASH LAW, P.O. Box 245, Beverly, WV 26253

A graduate of the National School of Basketmaking in West Germany, Rachel Nash Law also studied at the International School of Interior Design in Washington, D.C. and earned a B.S. from Virginia Polytechnic Institute and State University in Blacksburg.

Law's baskets have been seen at the Renwick Gallery, Washington; Arrowmont School of Arts and Crafts, Contemporary Art Gallery, Louisville, Kentucky; Hightower Art Association, and in the 1984 television movie, "The Dollmaker."

She is a member of American Craft Council, Ohio Designer Craftsmen, and the Southern Highland Handicraft Guild. Recipients of a 1985 Appalachian Studies Fellowship, Law and colleague Cynthia Taylor are researching white oak basketry and writing a book on their findings.

## PATRICIA ANN LECHMAN, Department of Fine Arts, Shelby State Community College, P.O. Box 40568, Memphis, TN 38174

After receiving a B.S. from the University of Georgia, Patti Lechman earned an M.S. in design from Indiana University and an M.F.A. in ceramics from Michigan State University. She studied fiber at Penland School of Crafts and at Miami University.

Her works have been featured in Southern Accents,

American Craft, and are included in The Fiberarts Design Book II. Lechman received a first place award from The Basketry Link, a show organized by the publishers of The News Basket, and merit awards in the Tennessee Artist-Craftsmen's Biennial Exhibition and The Path of the Handweaver show in Memphis, Tennessee. She received the American Craft Council award at the Spotlight '83 show in Winston-Salem, North Carolina, and has exhibited in Fiber R/Evolution.

## KARI LØNNING, 36 Mulberry Street, Ridgefield, CT 06877

Kari Lønning earned a B.F.A. degree in ceramics from Syracuse University, and studied tapestry weaving in Sweden. She worked with cloth and wood before she turned exclusively to basketry.

Her work has shown at The Hand and Spirit Gallery, Scottsdale, Arizona; Detroit Gallery of Contemporary Art; Brookfield (Connecticut) Craft Center; The Kohler Arts Center, Sheboygan, Wisconsin; The Elements Gallery, Greenwich, Connecticut; and at the Pacific Basin School of Textile Arts.

In the 1985 Designed and Made for Use Competition at the American Craft Museum she received a design award. She was awarded a grant to study basketry by the Connecticut Commission on the Arts.

## DONA LOOK, P.O. Box 204, Algoma, WI 54201

Currently a partner in the Loeber/Look Studio, Dona Look is a self-taught basketmaker. Her work appeared in these shows: Art for the Table, an American Craft Council benefit in New York; Washington Craft Show, Smithsonian Institution; Basketry Today, an invitational traveling exhibit; Crafts/National, Buffalo; Fiber Individualists, Wustum Museum of Fine Arts in Racine, Wisconsin; Designed and Made for Use, American Craft Museum, New York.

She won first prize in the 1984 Philadelphia Craft Show at the Philadelphia Museum of Art. Look was featured in the portfolio section of American Craft magazine.

## JOHN MCQUEEN, RD 1, Box 119A, Alfred Station, NY 14803

After earning an M.F.A. from Tyler School of Art, Temple University, John McQueen received a National Endowment for the Arts grant. In 1980, he was a Japan-United States Friendship Commission Exchange fellow.

His group exhibits include Fiberwork of the Americas and Japan, Kyoto, Japan; The Contemporary Basketmaker, Purdue University; The New Basket—A Vessel for the Future, Potsdam, New York; The Art Fabric: Mainstream Exhibition, San Francisco; and the 1986 Inaugural Exhibition at the American Craft Museum in New York. He has had solo shows at galleries across the country, including the Hadler/Rodriguez Galleries, New York; Helen Drutt Gallery, Philadelphia; and Fiberworks Center for the Textile Arts, Berkeley, California. A collaborative installation with Jessie Shefrin was mounted at the Kohler Art Center in 1986.

McQueen has lectured and taught at schools and museums throughout North America, the Textile Museum, the Cleveland Museum of Art, Nova Scotia College of Art and Design, and the Art Institute of Chicago.

**MARY MERKEL-HESS**, 1110 Cottonwood Ave., Iowa City, IA 52240

Mary Merkel-Hess earned degrees from Marquette University, the University of Wisconsin-Milwaukee, and the University of Iowa.

She has exhibited throughout the United States, and won awards in Paper/Fiber VII, Johnson County (Iowa) Arts Center; The Basketry Link, Mendocino (California) Art Center; Fiber 83/Off the Loom, Rock Island, Illinois; and Banc Iowa Invitational Art Fair, Cedar Rapids, Iowa.

Merkel-Hess had solo exhibits in 1985 at Middle Tennessee State University and the Iowa Artisans Gallery in Iowa City.

**NORMA MINKOWITZ**, 25 Broad View Road, Westport, CT 06880

A Cooper Union Art School graduate, Norma Minkowitz has been a professional fiber artist since 1972. She has lectured and taught throughout the eastern United States.

Her work has been shown in numerous exhibitions, including The Great American Foot, Clothing To Be Seen, and Baroque '74, all at the Museum of Contemporary Crafts, New York; Fibre Structures, Pittsburgh; The Flexible Medium: Art Textiles from the Museum Collection, the Renwick Gallery, Washington; Second International Competition of Miniature Fibre Work, British Craft Centre, London; and Fiber R/Evolution, Milwaukee. She has had a number of solo exhibitions at Julie: Artisans' Gallery, New York.

Her work has appeared in periodicals such as *American Craft, Hartford Magazine*, and *Fiberarts Magazine*, and in a number of books: *Textile Collector's Guide* (Monarch), *The Container Book* (Crown), *Design Principles and Problems* (Holt, Rinehart & Winston), and *Contemporary Crafts of the Americas* (Regnery).

Minkowitz has received awards from New Britain Museum of American Art, Wesleyan University, Convergence '76, Penn State University, and Pittsburgh Center for the Arts. She was first place winner in fiber in ArtQuest '86, at Parsons School of Design in New York, and she placed first in Objects and Images In-Of-Under-About Surface at the Monterey Peninsula (California) Museum of Art.

**RINA PELEG**, 640 Broadway, Apt. 8E, New York, NY 10012

Rina Peleg's work is represented in the collections of the Greenville County (South Carolina) Museum of Art, the Ceramic Museum, Tel Aviv, Alfred University, and in other institutions. She has been featured in *Kunst & Handwerk, Ceramics Monthly, American Ceramics*, and *Fiberarts* magazines.

Peleg has exhibited in group shows, including Westwood Clay National, Los Angeles; Basketwork, Renwick Gallery Anniversary, Washington; and the 40th International Ceramic Art exhibition, Faenza, Italy. She has had solo shows at the Ceramics Museum in Tel Aviv, the Branch Gallery, Washington, Theo Portnoy Gallery and Heller Gallery in New York, and at the Everson Museum of Art in Syracuse.

Peleg studied at Bezalel Academy of Arts and Crafts in Jerusalem, and earned her M.F.A. from Alfred University. She taught ceramics at Haifa University and at the Teacher Training College for the Kibbutz Movement in Oranim.

**ED ROSSBACH**, 2715 Belrose Avenue, Berkeley, CA 94705

Ed Rossbach received a B.A. in painting and design from the University of Washington, holds an M.F.A. in ceramics and weaving from Cranbrook Academy of Art, and an M.A. in art education from Columbia University. His work is in the collections of the Museum of Modern Art, New York; Stedelijk Museum, Amsterdam; American Crafts Museum, New York; Renwick Gallery, Washington; Trondheim (Norway) Museum; The Brooklyn Museum. He has exhibited at Nouvelle Vannerie, Musee des Arts Decoratifs, Lausanne, Switzerland; the Triennale, Milan; the Brussels World's Fair; Museum of Contemporary Crafts, New York; Oakland (California) Art Gallery; Fiberworks Gallery, Berkeley, California; Fiber Constructions, The Textile Museum, Washington.

He has written three books on basketry: *The Nature of Basketry* (Schiffer Pub., Ltd.), *The New Basketry* (Van Nostrand Reinhold), and *Baskets as Textile Art* (Van Nostrand Reinhold). His articles have appeared in *American Craft, Craft Horizons, Handweaver*, and *Fiberarts* magazine.

Rossbach is Professor Emeritus of design at the University of California at Berkeley, and an Honorary Fellow of the American Craft Council.

**JANE SAUER**, 6332 Wydown Boulevard, St. Louis, MO 63105

Jane Sauer earned a B.F.A. from Washington University, and has been a full-time studio artist since 1979. She was artist-in-residence at New City School in St. Louis, and conducted workshops at Arrowmont School of Crafts, The Cleveland Museum of Art, Haystack Mountain School of Crafts, and at the Craft Alliance Art Center.

Sauer has had solo and two-person shows at The Hand and Spirit Gallery, Scottsdale, Arizona, The Works Gallery, Philadelphia, Gayle Wilson Gallery, Long Island, and B.Z. Wagman Gallery, St. Louis. Additional exhibitions include The New Basket: A

Vessel for the Future, a traveling exhibit; Other Baskets, Craft Alliance Gallery, St. Louis, and the Worcester (Massachusetts) Art Center; 4th International Exhibition of Miniature Textiles, British Crafts Centre, London.

The *St. Louis Dispatch, American Craft, Fiberarts Magazine, The Crafts Report*, and *The New York Times* are a few publications which have covered Sauer's work. She received the Best of Show award at the Maryland Crafts Council Juried National Biennial in 1986, and received a Visual Artist's grant from the National Endowment for the Arts.

**KARYL SISSON**, 1750 North Beverly Glen, Los Angeles, CA 90077

Karyl Sisson earned an M.F.A. from the University of California at Los Angeles, and a B.S. (magna cum laude) from New York University. She was a merit award winner in ArtQuest '86. Her work has appeared in Artists Craftsmen '82, Braithwaite Fine Arts Gallery, Cedar City, Utah; Fiber Structure National II, III, and IV, Downey (California) Museum of Art; Within and Beyond the Basket, Pacific Basin School of Textile Arts, Berkeley, California, and Fiber R/Evolution, Milwaukee, Wisconsin.

**KAREN TURNIDGE**, 1270 Denise Drive, Kent, OH 44240

Karen Turnidge studied at the University of Oregon and Kent State University. She attended numerous workshops on basketry techniques, metalworking, and jewelry making.

Exhibitions of her work include New Outlook/ Fibers, Kent State University; Best of '85 Ohio Designer Craftsmen, Contemporary Metals USA, Downey Museum of Art, Los Angeles; Basketry Today, an invitational traveling exhibition, and Crafts National, State University of New York, Buffalo. She received an award for jewelry design from Fashion Group Inc. in 1985.

**JAN YATSKO**, 313 E. Frederick Street, Lancaster, PA 17602

Jan Yatsko studied papermaking and basketmaking at Peter's Valley Craft School, Layton, New Jersey, and Mannings Handweaving School, East Berlin, Pennsylvania.

Yatsko's work has been featured in *The New York Times, Fiberarts* magazine, *The Goodfellow Catalog of Wonderful Things* (Berkeley), and *The Fiberarts Design Book II* (Lark Books).

Her exhibits include Basketry Form & Function, Los Angeles; Contemporary American Fibers, Reykjavik, Iceland; Basketry Invitational, Wilmette, Illinois; and the Winter Show, The Society of Arts and Crafts, Boston.